KB245654

Lectures on FTAs and RTAs

내일을여는지식 / 법 36

Lectures on FTAs and RTAs

Bong-Chul Kim

KSI 한국학술정보㈜

The phenomenon FTAs (or RTAs) is one of the prominent issues in the field of international economy or trade. More than one-half of world trade is performed by FTAs or RTAs. Recently, Korea and the other Northeast Asian countries opened their eyes to the new trend. For these reasons, this topic is becoming popular in the Northeast Asian society. These are also hot issues for national and international politics and economy in this Area.

Some of graduate or undergraduate schools already have the classes regarding this subject. The author has chosen some issues on FTAs or RTAs for the classes. The issues consist of 12 lectures in this book to understand the basic concepts of FTAs including RTAs. Therefore, the aim of this book is mainly to elucidate the meaning of the central principles on FTAs, RTAs or Regionalism. Especially, the lecture provides a vision for the CJK FTA in Northeast Asian region as a conclusion. This book is designed not as a reference work but as a practical teaching tool, for use by individuals or in research courses.

The author wish to express his gratitude to Professor Piet Eeckhout at King's College London (University of London) for his supervising the Ph.D thesis of the author. Many parts of this book are based on the thesis. He also thanks Professor Dong-Hoon Kim at Hankuk University of Foreign Studies for his critical review of the manuscript. He is one of the best mentors in the author's life.

Bong-Chul Kim
Seoul, Korea
November 2009

For lovely Sunny

CONTENTS

LECTURE 1
THE BASIC CONCEPTS CONCERNING MULTILATERALISM

1. The history of Multilateralism (ITO–GATT–Rounds–WTO)

The Bretton Woods Conference of 1944 recognised the need for an international institution to regulate trade as part of a larger plan for economic recovery after World War II. In 1945, the United States proposed to enter into negotiations for an **International Trade Organisation (ITO).** The negotiations on the General Agreement on Tariffs and Trade (GATT) also advanced well and signed in 1947. In 1948, the negotiations on the ITO Charter were completed in Havana. The Charter (the Havana Charter) for the establishment of the ITO set out the basic rules for international trade and economic matters. However, the Charter never entered into force and the ITO was never brought into being.

The Bretton Woods and the ITO

Without the ITO, countries had to try to handle the trade problems under **the GATT 1947**. Although it was not an organisation, the GATT gradually became the ocus for international governmental cooperationon

The GATT system

trade matters. the GATT system was the outcome of the failure of the ITO. GATT was formed in 1947 and lasted until 1994, when it was replaced by the World Trade Organisation. The main objective of the GATT was the reduction of barriers to international trade. This was achieved through the reduction of tariff barriers, quantitative restrictions and subsidies on trade through a series of agreements.

The GATT system held a total of **8 Rounds** and the history of the GATT can be divided into three phases: the first, from 1947 until the Torquay Round, largely concerned which commodities would be covered by the agreement and freezing existing tariff levels. A second phase, encompassing three rounds, from 1959 to 1979, focused on reducing tariffs. The third phase, consisting only of the Uruguay Round from 1986 to 1994, extended the agreement fully to new areas such as intellectual property, services, capital, and agriculture. Out of this Round the WTO was born. The GATT principles and agreements were adopted by the WTO.

(1) Geneva Round — 1947

The first Round resulted in 45,000 tariff concessions. The group of the Round had expanded to 23 by the time the negotiation was signed in 1947. The GATT was born with the Round.

(2) Annecy Round — 1949

The second Round took place in 1949 in Annecy, France. 13 countries took part in the round. The main focus of the talks was more tariff reductions, around 5000 total.

(3) Torquay Round — 1951

The third Round occurred in Torquay, England in 1951. 38 countries took part in the round. 8,700 tariff concessions were made totaling the remaining amount of tariffs to three-fourths of the tariffs which were in effect in 1948. The contemporaneous rejection by the United States of the Havana Charter signified the establishment of the GATT as a governing world body.

(4) Geneva Round — 1955–1956

The fourth Round returned to Geneva in 1955 and lasted until May 1956. 26 countries took part in the round. $2.5 billion in tariffs were eliminated or reduced.

(5) Dillon Round — 1960–1961

The fifth Round occurred once more in Geneva and lasted from 1960 to 1962. The talks were named after U.S. Treasury Secretary and former Under Secretary of State, Douglas Dillon, who first propoSecrthe talks. 26 countries took part in the round. Along with ry and foover $4.9 billion in tariffs, it ando yieles tdiscussion relamore io the creation of the Eurlioan Economic Community (EEC).

(6) Kennedy Round — 1964–1967

The sixth Round was the last to take place in Geneva from 1964 until 1967 and was named after the late US President Kennedy in his memory. 62 countries took part in the Round. Concessions were made on $40 billion worth of tariffs. Some of the GATT negotiation rules were also more clearly defined.

(7) Tokyo Round — 1973–1979

Reduced tariffs and established new regulations aimed at controlling the proliferation of non—tariff barriers and voluntary export restrictions. 102 countries countries took part in the round. Concessions were made on $190 billion worth.

(8) Uruguay Round — 1986–1994

The Uruguay Round began in 1986. It was the most ambitious round to date, hoping to expand the competence of the GATT to important new areas such as services, capital, intellectual property, textiles, and agriculture. 123 countries took part in the Round.

The GATT Rounds

Year	Place / Name	Subject	Countries
1947	Geneva	Tariffs	23
1949	Annecy	Tariffs	13
1951	Torquay	Tariffs	38
1956	Geneva	Tariffs	26
1960 ~1961	Geneva / Dillon Round	Tariffs	26
1964 ~1967	Geneva / Kennedy Round	Tariffs / Antidumping measures	62
1973 ~1979	Geneva / Tokyo Round	Tariffs / Non—tariffs measures / Framework Agreements	102
1986 ~1994	Geneva / Uruguay Round	Tariffs / Non—tariff measures / Rules / Services / Intellectual property / Dispute settlement / Textiles / Agriculture / Creation of WTO	123

2. WTO Agreements as Multilateral Trade Agreements

The idea of multilateralism emerged after the Second World War. **Multilateralism** was grounded on the MFN principle which was embedded in the GATT 1947 to institutionalise the multilateral trading system.

The Multilateralism

The WTO succeeded the GATT as the international organisation principally responsible for the multilateral regulation of trade. The rules of the WTO are the mostambitious and comprehensive multilateral trade laws ever ratified by member states and they provide an anchor and a set of norms for all members. The WTO is the result of the Uruguay Round of multilateral trade negotiations that began in Punta del Este, Uruguay, in September 1986 and culminate with approval of a Final Act on 15 December 1993. The agreements embodied in the Final Act were signed by the GATT Contracting Parties on 15 April 1994.

The WTO as the Multilateral organisation

The Final Act covers all the negotiating areas with two important exceptions. The first is the result of the 'market access negotiations' in which individual countries have made binding commitments to reduce or eliminate specific tariffs and non—tariff barriers to merchandise trade. These concessions are to be recorded in national schedules which will form an integral part of the Final Act. The second is the 'initial commitments' on liberalisation of trade in services. These commitments on liberalisation are also to be recorded in national schedules.

The Final Act

Although the legal texts of the results of the Uruguay Round consist of about 60 agreements, annexes,

The WTO Agreements

decisions and understandings. **The Agreements** fall into a structure of 6 parts such as:

- The Agreement Establishing the WTO
- The GATT 1994
- The GATS
- The TRIPS Agreement
- The Agreement on Dispute settlement
- The Agreement on Trade policy reviews.

The Agreement Establishing the WTO entered into force on 1 January 1995. The Agreement formally constitutes the WTO as an international organisation. Although the WTO has been faced with many challenges, it is now up and running successfully as a multilateral international organisation. The WTO Agreements include **the GATT** and its related interpretative decisions and understandings. The WTO Agreements also include the General Agreement on Trade in Services **(GATS)** and the Agreement on Trade–Related Aspects of Intellectual Property Rights **(TRIPS Agreement).** The WTO Agreements also incorporate an **Understanding on Dispute Settlement** that works significant changes to the GATT 1947 dispute settlement procedure.

At the highest level of generality, the WTO establishes **the basic framework** of the liberal and rules–based multilateral trading system. It has as its overarching goal the progressive elimination of barriers to the trade of goods and services with a view to encouraging an optimal allocation of global resources. It seeks to accomplish this goal by the establishment of certain

The Basic Framework for Multilateralism

fundamental rules such as the MFN principle and the
National Treatment principle.

3. Chronology of the WTO

- October 1947: 23 countries sign the General Agreement on
  Tariffs and Trade (GATT) in Geneva, Switzerland, to try to
  give an early boost to trade liberalisation.

- November 1947: Delegates from 56 countries meet in
  Havana, Cuba, to start negotiating the charter of a proposed
  International Trade Organisation (ITO).

- January 1, 1948: **GATT** 1947 comes into force.

- March 1948: Charter of the ITO signed but US Congress
  rejects it, leaving GATT as the only international instrument
  governing world trade.

- 1949: Second GATT Round of trade talks held at Annecy,
  France.

- 1950: Third GATT Round held in Torquay, England.

- 1956: The Geneva Round completed in May 1956, resulting in $2.5 billion in tariff reductions.

- 1960–1962: Fifth GATT Round named in honor of the 57th secretary of the United States Department of the Treasury Douglas Dillon who proposed the negotiations.

- 1964–1969: The Kennedy Round, named in honour of the late US president, achieves tariff cuts worth $40 billion of world trade.

- 1973–1979: The Seventh Round, launched in Tokyo, Japan, results in reducing not only tariffs but trade barriers as well

- 1986–1994: GATT trade ministers launch the Uruguay Round in Punta Del Este, Uruguay, embarking on the most ambitious and far–reaching trade round so far.

- 1986–1994: GATT negotiations culminate in the Marrakech Agreement that establishes the World Trade Organization (WTO).

- January 1, 1995: The WTO came into existence.

- December 9/13, 1996: The inaugural ministerial conference takes

place in Singapore. Disagreements between largely developed and developing economies emerge during this conference over four issues initiated by this conference, which led to them being collectively referred to as the "Singapore issues".
- May 18/20 1998: Second Ministerial Conference in Geneva, Switzerland.

- November 30/December 3, 1999: The Third Ministerial Conference takes place in Seattle, USA. The conference itself ends in failure, with massive demonstrations and riots (At least 30,000 protesters disrupt the summit) drawing worldwide attention.

- November 9/13, 2001: The Fourth Ministerial Conference takes place in Doha, Qatar. WTO members agree on the Doha Development Agenda (DDA or just Doha Round), the ninth Round which is intended to open negotiations on opening markets to agricultural, manufactured goods, and services. The Conference issues the Doha Declaration.

- December 11, 2001: China joins the WTO after 15 years of negotiations (the longest in GATT history).

- January 1, 2002: Taiwan joins under the name "Separate Customs Territory of Taiwan, Penghu, Kinmen and Matsu".

- August 2002: WTO rules in favour of the EU in its row with the US government over tax breaks for US exporters. The EU gets the go—ahead to impose $4 billion in sanctions against the US, the highest damages ever awarded by the WTO.

- September 1, 2002: Former Thai deputy prime minister Supachai Panitchpakdi begins a three—year term as director—general. He is the first WTO head to come from a developing nation.

- September 2003: WTO announces deal aimed at giving developing countries access to cheap medicines, hailing it as historic. Aid agencies express disappointment at the deal.

- September 10/14, 2003: 5th ministerial conference in Cancún, Mexico aims at forging agreement on the Doha round. An alliance of 22 southern states, the G20 (led by India, People's Republic of China and Brazil), resisted demands from the North for agreements on the so—called "Singapore issues", on competition policy and on public procurement in trad so—lks. Instead, they called for an end to agricultural subsidies within the EU and the US. The talks broke down without progress, although trade facilitation, one of the Singapore issues, re—emerged with the support from both developed and developing countries in later Doha Round discussion.

- December 2003: WTO rules that duties imposed by the US on imported steel are illegal. US President George W. Bush repeals the tariffs to avoid a trade war with the EU.

- August 2004: Geneva talks achieve a framework agreement on the Doha round. Developed countries will lower agricultural subsidies, and in exchange the developing countries will lower tariff barriers to manufactured goods.

- March 2005: Upholding a complaint from Brazil, WTO rules that US subsidies to its cotton farmers are illegal.

- May 2005: Paris talks aimed at finalizing issues for agreement before the December 2005 Ministerial Conference in Hong Kong are hung over technical issues. The group of five (U.S., Australia, the EU, Brazil and India) fail to agree over chicken, beef and rice. France continues to protest restrictions on subsidies to farmers. Oxfam accuses the EU of delaying tactics which threaten to scupper the Doha Round.

- October 2005: US offers to make big cuts in agricultural subsidies if other countries, notably EU do the same.

- November 11, 2005: WTO General Council successfully adopts Saudi Arabia's terms of Accession

- December 13/18, 2005: World trade talks in Hong Kong begin amid widespread belief that they will not succeed in making a breakthrough.

- July 24, 2006: At the end of yet another futile gathering of trade ministers in Geneva, Pascal Lamy formally suspends the negotiations.

- October 2006: The US and Russia reach agreement in principle on a bilateral market access deal in the context of Russia's efforts to join the WTO.

- January 11, 2007: Vietnam becomes the 150th WTO member state.

LECTURE 2
THE BASIC CONCEPTS CONCERNING REGIONALISM AND REGIONAL TRADE AGREEMENTS

1. Questions on Regionalism

The phenomenon of Regionalism is prominent in today's international trading system. Now, roughly more than one-half of world trade is performed under the preferential treatments of RTAs. Although the coverage and depth of preferential treatment varies from one RTA to another, the bases and concepts of **RTAs** can be contrasted against multilateral trade agreements.

Although there are still positive and negative opinions on Regionalism and Regional Trade Agreements, many countries have various kinds of RTAs. Why do they want to be engaged in RTA relationships? What are the effects of the phenomenon? What are the mainstreams of RTAs in the international economy or world trade? Many questions appear in relation to RTAs.

The phenomenon of Regionalism

Questions and issues on Regionalism and Regional Trade

The networks of RTAs are overlapping and their map Agreements is becoming more complicated with the proliferation of RTAs. Here, several issues are emerging regarding the linkages or the conflicts between RTAs and the WTO in different legal aspects. Why does the WTO want to regulate RTAs? How does the WTO regulate RTAs? What are the problems of and prospects for the issues?

2. Regionalism and Regional Trade Agreements

Regionalism is described in the Dictionary of Trade The Policy Terms, as "actions by governments to liberalise Concepts or facilitate trade on a regional basis, sometimes through free trade areas or customs unions." In the WTO context, **Regional Trade Agreements** (RTAs) have both a more general and a more specific mea—ning: more general, "because RTAs may be agreements concluded between countries not necessarily belonging to the same geographical region"; more specific, "beca—use the WTO provisions relate directly to conditions of preferential trade liberalisation with RTAs." Therefore, RTAs can be defined here in accordance with the terms of the WTO as 'any types of trade agreements between two or more customs territories within or across regions where the trade barriers are reduced or eliminated.'

RTAs are a major and perhaps irreversible feature Preferential of today's multilateral trading system. The number of trade under RTAs as well as the world share of preferential trade RTA by RTAs has been steadily increasing over the last systems of world trade decade. The quantification of **the share of preferential trade** in total trade may be seen as an indicator of the importance of the move towards RTAs world–wide. Before the WTO regime, preferential trade under RTA systems already represented 40% of world trade in the period 1988–1992. It increased to 42% during the period 1993–1997. In 2005, RTAs surveyed accounted for about 52.5% of global merchandise import flows. Now, roughly more than one–half of world trade is performed under the preferential tariff rates of RTAs.

The Share of the trade under the RTAs systems

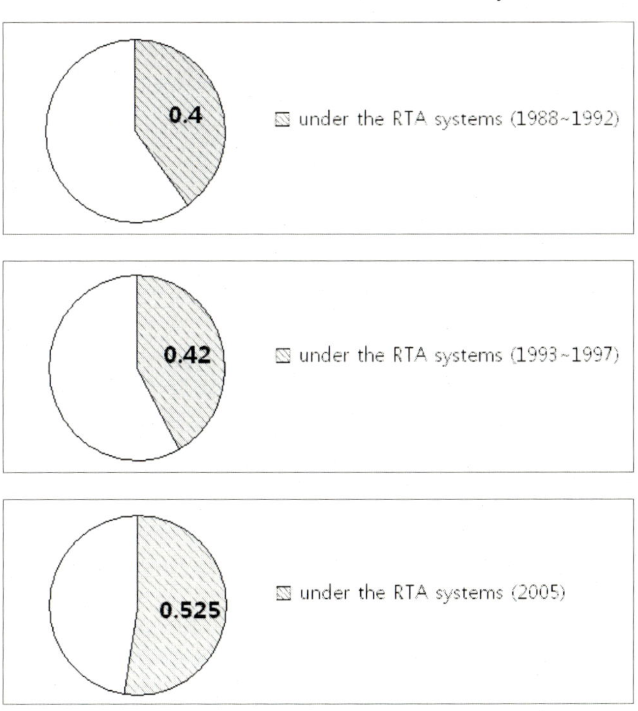

The principles or characteristics of the multilateral trade agreements such as many agreements in the WTO system and RTAs are different. Based on the principle of **non—discrimination**, all members of a multilateral trade agreement are bound to grant as favourable treatment to each other as they give to any other member, for example, **MFN status**. However, the trade in an RTA system is based on the principle of **discrimination**. Countries within a economic bloc under an RTA share **special preferences** not granted to countries outside the RTA.

The basic ideas of a multilateral trade agreement normally include **economic liberalism, multilateralism** and the principle of free trade based on comparative advantage. By contrast, basic ideas of an RTA include **economic regionalism, bilateralism or nationalism.** The trade in an RTA system is often based on strategic trade theory and neo—mercantilism. These different bases and principles can operate in the two systems. The system of a multilateral trade agreement is designed as a community open to all who are willing to follow membership rules. This is because the goal of multilateral trade agreements is to build a **unified and integrated global system** such as the WTO regime. By contrast, the system of an economic bloc under an RTA may function as an **exclusive club** that generates a 'them versus us' psychology. However, in the view of some advocates, regional economic blocs are also a way of building a stronger multilateral system in the long run.

The coverage and depth of preferential treatment varies from one RTA to another. Modern RTAs, and not exclusively those linking the most developed economies, tend to go far beyond tariff–cutting exercises. They provide for **increasingly complex regulations** governing intra–RTA trade with preferential rules of origin and they often also provide for a preferential regulatory framework for mutual services trade. The most sophisticated RTAs go beyond traditional trade policy mechanisms, to include regional rules on competition, intellectual property, investment, environment and labour.

The basic ideas of RTAs

3. The Motivations for Regional Trade Agreements

Basically supported by the positive opinions on Regionalism, the formation of RTAs is driven by **a variety of factors** that include economic, political and security considerations. The conclusion of RTAs may be driven by the search for access to larger markets,

A variety of factors for the motivations

which might be easier to engineer at the regional level, particularly in the absence of a willingness among WTO members to liberalise further on a multilateral basis.

Slow progress in multilateral trade negotiations under the Doha Round appears to have accelerated further the rush to forge RTAs. That is to say, the setback of negotiations at the WTO Ministerial Conference in Cancún apparently precipitated the forging of more RTA partnerships. Some countries argue that their participation in Regionalism provides a competitive spur to liberalisation at the multilateral level by promoting trade liberalisation on multiple fronts, while others may increasingly be drawn into RTAs for defensive reasons, as a mean of maintaining market access opportunities in the absence of MFN principle—driven liberalisation. These activities have intensified across all world regions particularly in the Western Hemisphere and Asian—Pacific.

Many countries can also use RTAs as **a vehicle for promoting deeper integration** of their economies than is presently available through the WTO, particularly for **issues that are not fully dealt with multilateral ways** This deeper integration covers RTA provisions dealing with product and market regulations such as **standards** and **competition policies, environment** and **labour.** Furthermore, it reaches the area of property rights such as protection of **intellectual property,** other intangible assets as well as physical and financial **investments** as. Particularly with regards to trade in services, preferential access by an RTA may enable a supplier to steal an irreversible march on the competition. Discriminatory liberalisation might also be attractive for countries that seek to reap gains from trade in product areas where they cannot compete internationally.

Smaller or developing countries particularly would see RTAs as a **defensive necessity,** while even larger or developed economies may turn to RTAs to avoid being left out in the cold. Developing countries have been active in preferential liberalisation by RTAs, particularly since the Uruguay Round. Some RTAs provide special rules favouring small or developing countries. Many of these RTAs involve developed countries but several other RTAs are among developing countries. Even the WTO provides the Enabling Clause for the regulation of the RTAs amongst developing countries. They believe that regional economic cooperation by RTAs permits countries to overcome constraints posed by the relatively small size of their individual markets and the low purchasing power in their economies. Integrating smaller economies into larger regional economic space expands the size of the market and facilitates cost reduction through economies of scale and scope. Therefore, RTAs provide developing countries a breathing space in which to adapt both their economies and policies to the global market place. Many RTAs amongst developing countries have a **positive impact** on their members' intra–trade.

Membership in RTAs is also thought to provide a means of securing **foreign direct investment,** particularly for a country with low labour costs that has preferential access to larger, more developed market. The case of Mexico's investment inflows in the wake of its membership in the NAFTA is a case in point. Developing countries, in particular, might be willing to forego the benefits conferred by Generalised System of Preferences (GSP) programmes and instead commit themselves to signing reciprocal RTAs to developed countries in order to secure access to their markets; such a strategy is usually deemed to have strong signalling effect and act as a pull for foreign investment. Thus, RTAs may perform a sort of dual locking function, locking–out competition and locking in investment.

Political considerations are also reported to be a key to the decision to foster RTAs. Governments seek to consolidate peace and increase regional security with their RTA partners, or to increase their bargaining power in multinational negotiations by securing commitment first on a regional basis, or as a means to demonstrate good governance and to prevent backsliding on political and economic reforms. Larger countries trying to forge new geographical alliances and cement diplomatic ties, thus ensuring or rewarding political support by providing increased discriminatory access to a larger market, may also use them. The US–Israel FTA was no doubt motivated more by political and military concerns than economic concerns.

4. The effect of Regional Trade Agreements

Regionalism or RTAs can be detected as one of the dimensions in a curious phenomenon concerning the way in which governments operate as partners of the agreements. It seems that government constituents or citizens are not always happy with a notion of applicable and significant government activities always applying at one level, such as the 'nation–state.' Clearly this creates perplexing conceptual questions for international (economic and national) law, including issues of 'statehood', allocation of powers, dominion over land and minerals, ideas of 'citizenship', concepts of state succession (such as related to sovereign debts), and many more. Although **the sovereignty issue** may emerge in the WTO stage as a multilateral rule, the developing complexity of gradations of 'independence' or 'sovereignty' by RTAs also challenges some of the established notions of international law.

Gradations of sovereignty by RTAs

Regarding this issue, the WTO Panel on the Turkey – Restrictions on Imports of Textile and Clothing Products case ruled that unless an institution under a certain RTA is provided with distinct rights and obligations, and therefore has a legal personality, each party to the RTA remains accountable for measures it adopts for application to its specific territory. Nevertheless, the legal standing of WTO Members which become parties to a customs union seems less clear.

The opinion of the WTO Panel regarding the issue

The effects of RTAs on the parties and on the multilateral trading system as a whole are manifold and **positive or negative aspects of the effects** are in

Positive or negative aspects of

evidence. First of all, although liberalisation through RTAs is generally held to be a **second—best option**, it may be the only option if there is resistance to liberalisation at the multilateral level. Furthermore, RTAs can be the **functions of laboratories** for some countries with regards the adoption of new trade disciplines at the multilateral level. Some would argue that the negotiation of RTAs provides countries with valuable negotiating skills for multilateral negotiation stages.

However, there is ample evidence to suggest that the negotiation and administration of multilateral agreements strains the institutional capacity of even the largest countries and may dampen enthusiasm for liberalisation at the multilateral level. RTAs create vested interests determined to avoid the dilution of preferential margins, while labyrinthine rules of origin make international trade more costly and complex. Moreover, RTAs may pose a threat to a balanced development of world trade through increased trade and investment diversion, particularly if liberalisation on a preferential basis is not accompanied by concurrent MFN principle liberalisation. Since RTAs are preferential and discriminatory by nature, their unchecked multiplication seriously fragments world trade by attacking the MFN principle, which is the backbone of the multilateral trading system. Therefore, the preferential and discriminatory treatment of RTAs can be one of the **causes of the erosion of MFN principle in multilateral trading systems** such as the WTO.

5. Different Stages of RTAs

Regional integration tends to involve several different types by the stages of development: (1) Free Trade Area or Free Trade Agreement **(FTA)**; (2) Customs Union **(CU)**; (3) Common Market **(CM)**; (4) Monetary Union **(MU)**; and (5) Political Union **(PU)**.

The stages of development

Different Stages of RTAs

A **free trade agreement** (FTA) is an agreement in the form of freer access to the main market. In the FTA, tariffs between the members are basically eliminated, but they keep their original tariffs against other non-member (third) countries. That is to say, each country **retains its own tariff structure against outsiders.** In the **customs union** (CU) stage, however, member states set up common external tariff (CET) against non-member (third) countries, in addition to eliminating tariffs among themselves. Furthermore,

FTAs and CUs

although some FTAs may try to do, many RTAs in the customs union stage construct common trade remedy rules against the third countries. Some of them even abolish these rules for intra–RTA trade. To sum up, a customs union is a **'freer trade agreement' with common external trade policies.**

One of the central issues for countries planning to integrate their trade by an RTA is whether to choose an FTA or customs union. The great advantage of a customs union is that, because members have a common external trade rules, it is possible to have much simpler internal border formalities. In contrast, an FTA leaves external trade policy to individual member governments, and faces a problem known as 'trade deflection.'

The differences between FTAs and CUs

FTA stage

FTA

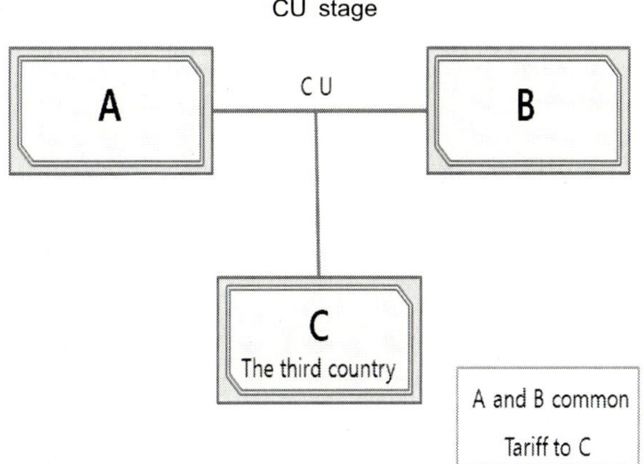

A **common market** (CM) is the next step following CM
a customs union, which addresses not only **removal
of border tariffs and setting up common external
trade rules** against third countries, but also aims at
removing internal non–tariff barriers such as trade
remedy measures to free movement of resources.
The goal of this form of RTAs is to remove non–tariff
barriers in the form of physical, fiscal, and technological
obstacles, and thereby create a unified economic
market in order to achieve a higher of productivity and
standard of living higher than that of a customs union.

CM stage

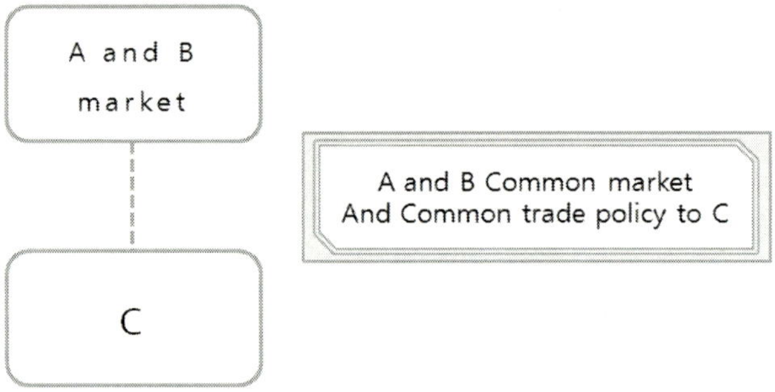

A and B
market

A and B Common market
And Common trade policy to C

C

The final stages are a monetary and political union. MU and PU The **monetary union** (MU) involves the establishment of a **common currency**, which we have just witnessed. **Political union** (PU) entails the **merging of governments** with respect to legislative, judicial and administrative activities, among others.

In practice, RTAs are often a combination of these ideal types. Many fail to conform to the definitions. For example, contingent protection often remains applicable to intra–RTA trade, implying that internal trade is not truly free.

6. Is it a 'spaghetti-bowl' or a 'carrot'? - Two opinions on Regional Trade Agreements

There may be **negative and positive opinions on Regionalism and RTAs.** The negative opinion argues that as RTAs spread, the world trade system comes to look like a **'spaghetti-bowl'** of ever more complicated trade barriers, each depending on the supposed 'nationality' of products (determined by ever more complex and arbitrary rules of origin). This opinion warns that RTAs pose a 'deadly threat to the multilateral system', and that they 'have become a vehicle for the introduction of extraneous issues into the WTO for the benefit of certain countries' narrow domestic interests'. This opinion views RTAs as **undermining the MFN principle and distorting the role of the WTO.**

The increase in RTAs has produced the phenomenon of **overlapping membership of RTAs.** Because each RTA will tend to develop its own regime for intra-RTA trade, the coexistence in a single country of differing trade rules applying to different RTA partners has become a frequent feature. According to the negative opinion on RTAs, this can hamper trade flows merely by the costs involved for traders in meeting multiple sets of trade rules. Furthermore, the proliferation of RTAs, especially as their scope broadens to includes policy areas not regulated multilaterally, increases the risks of inconsistencies in the rules and procedures among RTAs themselves, and between RTAs and the multilateral framework. This is likely to give rise to regulatory confusion, distortion of regional markets, and severe implementation problems, especially where there are overlapping RTAs.

By contrast, the **positive opinion** argues that RTAs can serve as **carrots** to encourage the spread of political and economic freedom by breaking down barriers to trade between countries. It notes that as membership of the WTO grows, reaching consensus multilaterally becomes more difficult and RTAs may provide a template for broader negotiations, particularly in politically sensitive sectors including labour and environmental standards. For example, advocates of RTAs cite the gains to be had from economies of scale, competition and the attraction of foreign direct investment on the basis of positive opinion. They insist that the global economy is enjoying a period of sustained and widely distributed economic growth, suggesting that RTAs are not an immediate economic threat. The motivations for Regionalism are normally based on the positive opinions on RTAs.

Both the negative and the positive opinions are partially true. That is to say, the proliferation of RTAs presents WTO members with opportunities and challenges at the same time. The opportunity is to use them as experimental laboratories for cooperation on issues that have not been addressed multilaterally, especially issues where the outcome is applied on an MFN basis in the WTO stage. The promotion of free trade through RTAs can foster trade liberalisation and benefit economic development by integrating countries into the world economy. However, the challenge is to control the discrimination that is inherent in RTAs. The development of complex networks of non—MFN trade relations in RTAs will increase discrimination and may well undermine transparency and predictability in international trade relations.

Therefore, multilateral economic systems such as the WTO have the key to ensure that RTAs are designed and implemented in order to complement and not undermine the multilateral trade regime. 'Multilateralising Regionalism' is one of the possible routes which multilateral trade systems can take.

'Multilateralising Regionalism'

Negative and Positive opinions on RTAs

Negative Opinion	Positive Opinion
• Spaghetti boul theory	• Carrot theory
• RTAs threat MTAs	• RTAs encourage MTAs
• Complicated trade rules	• Breaking down trade barriers

LECTURE 3
THE TRENDS OF REGIONAL TRADE AGREEMENTS

1. The analysis of Regional Trade Agreements by type of agreement

In the GATT period 1948–1994, the GATT received **124 notifications of RTAs** relating to trade in goods, and since the creation of the WTO in 1995, more than **250 additional RTAs** covering trade in goods or services have been notified. The surge in RTAs has continued unabated since the early 1990s. If the RTAs currently being negotiated, at a proposal stage and those signed but not yet in force are implemented by 2010, the number of RTAs in force will be **close to 400**. In part, the increase in notifications is a reflection of increased WTO membership and new notification obligations. However, it is obvious that the rate of growth of RTAs is continuing unabated.

The number of RTAs

Turning to the typology of RTAs in force, the most common category is FTA, which account for over 90% of all RTAs in force, customs unions account for less than 10%, respectively. The **predominance of FTAs over customs unions** is probably due to the fact that they are faster to conclude and require the lower degree of policy coordination among the parties since in an FTA each party maintains its own trade policy. Customs unions, on the other hand, require the establishment of common external tariff and harmonisation of external trade policies, implying a greater loss of autonomy over the parties' commercial policies and longer and more complex negotiations and implementation periods. Therefore, FTAs are easier to negotiate than customs unions.

Bilateral agreements account for over 80% of all RTAs notified and in force and for almost 90% of those under negotiation. This is because many countries feel that bilateral agreements are easier to negotiate than plurilateral agreements. Bilateral agreements may include more than two countries when one of them is an RTA itself. A noteworthy development expected in the near future, which reflects the growing consolidation of established trading relationships, is the emergence of new category of agreement, namely RTAs where each party is a distinct RTA itself. The fact that several such RTAs have been under negotiation for some time, but that none, thus far, has been concluded suggests that such RTAs are complex to negotiate.

type of agreement

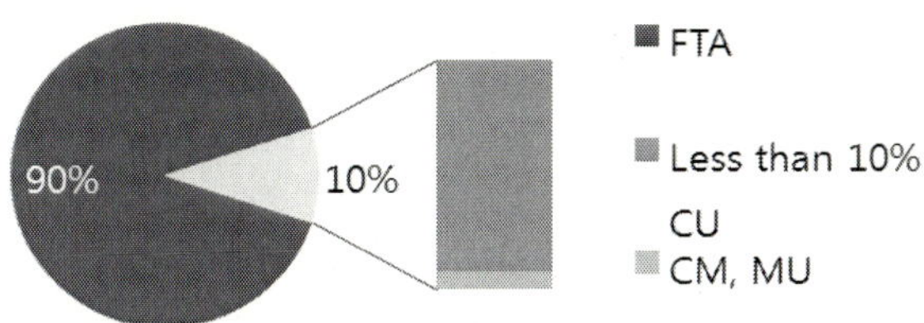

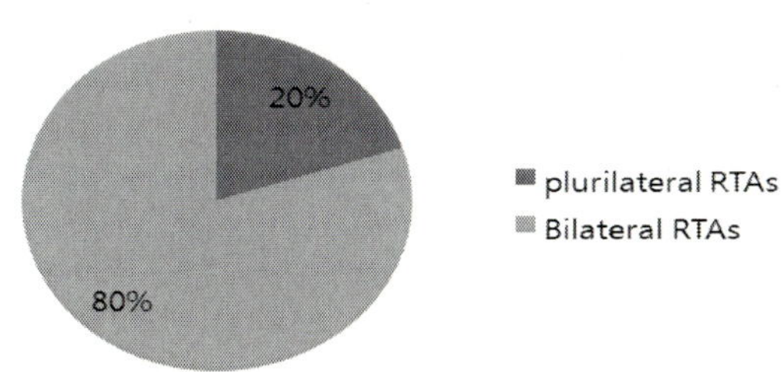

Most **FTA** parties focus their attention on **strategic market access** or **strategic political alliances**. They are often unbound by geographical considerations. These considerations appear to be particularly relevant to the current wave of cross–regional FTAs. In **customs unions**, on the other hand, **geographical considerations** play a pivotal role in defining the objective of economic and often political integration among the parties concerned. As for membership in partial scope agreements, their limited trade coverage,

Causes — strategic market access, strategic political alliances, geographical considerations, etc.

poor implementation record and scarce visibility, make them much less attractive to countries, including developing ones, which are committed to comprehensive trade liberalisation.

The configuration of RTAs is diverse and becoming increasingly complex with overlapping RTAs and networks of RTAs spanning within and across the continents at regional and sub-regional levels. Countries are opting for simple RTA configurations, for example, two parties rather than the more burdensome plurilateral RTAs, which are more typical of customs unions.

2. Main characteristics of recent Regional Trade Agreements

Recent RTAs-related characteristics are apparent. First, countries across the world, including those traditionally reliant on multilateral trade liberalisation, are increasingly making RTAs the **centrepiece of their policy**. Although RTAs are on a par with multilateral trade objectives for some countries, RTAs have become the priority for many others. This indicates **a shift of resources** from multilateral trade objectives to the pursuance of RTAs in many cases.

Second, RTAs are **becoming increasingly complex**, in many cases establishing regulatory trade regimes which go beyond multilaterally agreed trade regulations. For example, many of the new RTAs cover liberalisation of trade in services. Furthermore, their outreach in

Recent RTAs-related characteristics — centrepiece of their policy, becoming increasingly complex, reciprocal preferential RTAs, expansion terms of partners is becoming both innovative and not geographically bound.

Third, **reciprocal preferential RTAs between developed and developing countries** are on the increase pointing to a decreasing reliance by some developing countries on non–reciprocal systems of preferences. That is to say, the geopolitics of RTAs indicates an increase in so–called North–South RTAs and their gradual replacement of long established non–reciprocal systems. It is also significant that the **emergence of RTAs among key developing countries such as BRICs** (Brazil, Russia, India and China). It may be evidence of a strengthening of so–called South–South trading patterns. The increasing number of South–South RTAs is normally based on several major RTA hubs such as MERCOSUR, ASEAN and SAFTA in the developing world.

Fourth, RTA dynamics show, in spite of regional idiosyncrasies, a **general pattern of expansion and consolidation.** On the one hand, we are witnessing a proliferation of intra–regional RTAs, which account for a large proportion of the total increase in RTAs. On the other hand, RTAs on a **continent–wide scale** are in the making. While the number of **intra–regional RTAs** has expanded in all regions, their consolidation into region–wide RTAs has made slow progress in some regions. Paradoxically, besides political differences and technical difficulties, this slow progress may be partly attributed to the proliferation of RTAs itself and in particular to **cross–regional RTAs.**

Traditionally, RTA formation occurred between so–called 'natural' trading partners, geographically

and consolidation, comprehensive in coverage and etc.

contiguous countries with already well–established trading patterns. Indeed most countries sign their first RTA with one or several neighbouring or regional partners. However, once a country has exhausted its strictly regional prospect, it may begin to look **further afield for RTA partners**. This trend is most evident in countries of the Western Hemisphere, Europe and increasingly Asia–Pacific.

In terms of their scope and depth, RTAs differ considerably with some providing for the exchange of tariff preferences on a limited range of products and others being **highly comprehensive in coverage and including wide–ranging trade regulatory regimes**. Given the requirements prescribed by the WTO provisions on RTAs, partial scope agreements falling under the legal cover of the Enabling Clause concern exclusively agreements among developing countries and in most cases they tend to have limited product coverage.

3. The two waves in history and the third wave of the proliferation

There have been **three waves in the trends of RTAs**. Based on the political theory of Regionalism, the trends in the past can be divided into two different waves. **The first wave of RTAs** appeared in the 1960s. This was made up primarily of **North–North and South–South RTAs**, the latter being generally

The three waves

recognised to have been less successful than the former. Different, primarily **North–South RTAs** appeared during the 1980s in a **second wave**. The proliferation of RTAs starting the late 1990s and the beginning of the 21th century as the third wave, has its roots in a combination of geopolitical developments most of which date back to the late 1980s or early 1990s.

These geopolitical developments include the uncertainty concerning the fate of the Uruguay Round, which prompted several countries to pursue preferential deals as an **insurance against an eventual failure of multilateral trade negotiations.** For example, the proliferation of the European RTAs to include new acceding countries from Central and Eastern Europe, the Balkans and the Mediterranean is still ongoing on the track of EU expansion.

The third wave — the insurance role

One of the most noteworthy developments in this respect is the **United States' shift** from reluctant to solid RTA player as reflected by its ambitious and aggressive RTA agenda. The United States has traditionally only turned to a robust RTA agenda when the WTO system has stalled in achieving further trade liberalisation. However, given the proliferation of RTAs, the United States has invested in reinvigorating its RTA agenda. Therefore, the policy debate in this country has moved to an **acceptance of the existence of RTAs** and a focus on mechanisms both within the WTO system and outside that system that might ensure that this robust RTA activity complements the WTO system.

The the policy shift of the United States

This favourable stance towards RTAs by the United States sparked a '**domino effect**' on decisions of other countries to pursue the policy of RTAs. The

The domino effect

United States' RTAs are the most far reaching in terms of achieving substantial change in other countries' social and economic policies by setting so—called 'US—friendly global standards' for investor privileges, environmental protection, workers' rights, intellectual property rights, deregulation of service industries and privatisation in general, wherever they are signed. For these reasons, many RTAs are sometimes classified into two large groups of RTA styles, the **European and the American styles.**

The policy of **'addictive Regionalism'** is pursued by countries such as Chile, Mexico and Singapore which have forged preferential relations with all their major trading partners. The fragmentation of the former Soviet Union and the disbandment of its related Council for Mutual Economic Assistance (COMECON) has led to a new cluster of RTAs between transition economies and the EU and the EFTA States as well as among transition economies themselves. The process of alignment with the EU and the re—establishment of forgone preferential trade relations by the transition economies is still ongoing and accounts for a major share of the notified RTAs in force in the 1990s.

The other major cluster of RTAs is the one consisting of **RTAs between developed and developing countries.** The EU and the EFTA States account for over half of these RTAs through the Euro—Mediterranean agreements with partner countries in North Africa and the Middle East and several other bilateral RTAs with countries such as Chile and Mexico. The United States is catching up having rapidly concluded several RTAs with developing country partners and with several more on its negotiating agenda. Other countries are following the lead of the EU and the United States. These include Japan, Korea, Australia, New Zealand and Canada, all of which are engaged in RTA negotiations with countries across the globe and particularly with South East Asian and Latin American countries.

The peculiarity of the RTAs falling under this category is that they are underpinned by criteria such as **reciprocity** and comprehensive trade liberalisation as opposed to the non–reciprocal systems of preferences enjoyed by these same countries under schemes like the Generalised System of Preferences (GSP) and other unilateral initiatives such as Cotonou and CARIBCAN which are under the legal cover of waivers granted by WTO Members. Under the existing WTO provisions on RTAs, the proliferation of RTAs between developed–developing countries poses the latter with the formidable challenge of transition from non–reciprocal trade preferences to trade liberalisation on a mutual basis under **reciprocal RTAs** with developed country partners. A case in point are the new RTAs between the EU and the African, Caribbean and Pacific group of countries (ACP) which are supposed to replace the existing non–reciprocal preferences of the Cotonou Agreement.

Reciprocal RTAs

LECTURE 4
THE MAP OF REGIONAL TRADE AGREEMENT
NETWORKS

1. Overview of the map and the networks

As the number of RTAs increases, **the map of** Becoming
RTA networks is becoming more complex. First of more
all, there are signs of consolidation of existing complex
agreements into larger RTAs in all world regions. The
EU is the best example of the interplay between RTA
expansion and consolidation. Furthermore, the EU is
not alone in pursuing sub-regional and continent-wide
economic integration. Latin American countries, for
instance, are actively pursuing both expansion of their
intra-RTA network and consolidation of existing
agreements. At a continental level, all countries of the
Western Hemisphere, with the exception of Cuba, are
participating in the establishment of the FTAA (Free
Trade Agreement of the Americas). In Asia, in recent
years there has been a revival of the idea of an East
Asian Community comprising ASEAN countries, Japan,

China and Korea. On a broader scale, RTAs developments in Asia–Pacific show India, Australia and New Zealand engaged in strengthening their economic ties with South East Asian countries.

In terms of geographic coverage, new regional developments have **changed the pattern of RTAs**. With only a few exceptions of cross–regional RTAs, many RTAs were intra–regional until the early 1990s. However, this is no longer true as researched above. This pattern does not show, at this point in time, that RTAs will develop into 'fortress' arrangements intended to lock out foreign trade. On the other hand, we can see the **'hub and spoke'** situation in the map of RTA networks. Both hubs and spokes may be countries or RTAs themselves. Many hubs may have multiple spokes and there are hubs now in all geographic areas of the world economy.

Change of the pattern

2. The two traditional pivots of RTAs – Europe and American Continent

RTAs have basically been developed in **two pivotal regions**. They are the European and American continents. **Europe** has the greatest concentration of RTAs with the **EU** and the **EFTA** representing the main continental hubs. Several factors account for the density of intra–European RTAs, all of which are linked to a certain extent to the ongoing expansion and consolidation intrinsic to the process of political

Europe – EU and EFTA

and economic integration of the continent.

The EU enlargement also consolidated the **extensive network of intra-European RTAs** built over the years by considerably reducing the number of existing RTAs. This process of expansion and consolidation is due to continue in the coming years as more countries are added to the list of candidates for EU accession. The process of Stabilisation and Association in South Eastern Europe adds further to the number of RTAs in Europe with the establishment of a network of bilateral agreements between the EU and these countries. A similar process is underway between the EU and countries in North Africa and the Middle East, with the aim to establish a Euro-Mediterranean Free Trade Area by 2010.

Further afield, the EU and the EFTA States are expanding their respective networks of RTAs. The EU is engaged in FTA negotiations with the countries of the GCC and with MERCOSUR members. Its negotiations on EPAs with Eastern and Southern Africa (ESA), the Caribbean Forum of ACP States (CARIFORUM), the Southern African Development Community (SADC) and the Pacific ACP States were officially commenced in 2004. The Caribbean is the only region that initialled a full EPA with the EU by 31 December 2007, the expiry date of the waiver covering the Cotonou trade preferences. In total, 35 ACP countries initialled either a full or an interim agreement by the end of 2007.

For almost ten years after 1997, the EU stuck to a moratorium on launching new negotiations on RTAs. With the exception of these ongoing negotiations, the EU has indicated that it will not negotiate any more

RTAs during the Doha Round. However, the EU has been signalling its desire to strengthen trade relations with South East Asian countries although no FTA between the EU and ASEAN has yet been announced. Furthermore, the EU finished the FTA negotiation with Korea. On the other hand, the EFTA States signed FTAs with Singapore and Korea.

Compared to Europe, RTA dynamics in the **American continent** are more heterogeneous in nature with several major players engaged in **multilayered RTA processes** and not necessarily sharing similar objectives. That is to say, two features have become evident at first sight from observing RTAs that have taken place in the Western Hemisphere. The first feature is the enthusiasm with which the countries of the region have embarked on negotiations of RTAs. The second salient feature of the recent trend in the Americas is the apparent unorganised and patchy way in which it has been evolving.

The North American Free Trade Agreement (**NAFTA**) is an FTA involving the United States, Canada and Mexico in **North America** and an expansion of the Canada–US FTA (CUSFTA). Although NAFTA led problems and resistances in the region, it built a huge free trade area and had a great impact on other RTAs in many ways. Furthermore, by strengthening the rules and procedures governing trade and investment on this continent, the NAFTA has allowed trade and investment flows in North America to skyrocket. Before 2000, the United States had only three comprehensive FTAs with Canada, Israel and Mexico including NAFTA. Having secured RTAs with Singapore, Chile and Jordan in 2003, the United States signed in 2004 FTAs with Australia and, several Central American countries as part of the Dominican Republic–Central American Free Trade Agreement (DR–CAFTA). In the Middle East region, the United States already signed FTAs with several countries or is in the negotiation stage as part of its drive to patch together an overall US–Middle East FTA by 2013. It also signed an FTA with Korea in East Asian region.

The other two NAFTA members have also been active. After FTAs with Chile and Israel in 1996, Canada signed FTAs with Costa Rica in 2001 and the EFTA in 2008. It is also in the stages of negotiations for more RTAs with many countries all over the world such as Singapore, Korea, the Caribbean Community (CARICOM) and the Dominican Republic. Mexico which has already signed RTAs with many countries all over the world such as Israel, the EU, the EFTA, Chile and Japan, is also intent on expanding its RTA network and is negotiating or considering more RTAs with many other countries.

RTA developments in **Latin America** suggest increasing efforts towards consolidation and deepening of the network of RTAs among South and Central American countries. Latin American countries share a cultural tradition that makes a difference to the market oriented RTAs being pursued by North American countries. The main RTA in this region is **MERCOSUR.** During the second half of the 1980s, negotiations started between Brazil and Argentina, the two major players in the South American region, concerning regional community integration. The negotiations resulted

The MERCOSUR in Latin America

in the 1991 Treaty of Asunción. The economically highly dependent countries of Uruguay and Paraguay also acceded. This is the base of the MERCOSUR. During the course of the 1990s, Bolivia and Chile became associated members based on an agreement concerning the free trade area with the MERCOSUR. Recently, Mexico has signalled its intention to apply for associate membership in the MERCOSUR.

The MERCOSUR members are working towards the objective of a full–fledged customs union or common market, and have concluded a framework agreement with three members of the Andean Community, which aims to the gradual establishment of a FTA. Brazil has already submitted a programme headed 'Objective 2006'. Its purpose may be compared to the operation for establishing the internal market in the EC in 1992. Argentina also has submitted a proposal for the establishment of a Monetary Institute for the MERCOSUR, with the idea of coordinating monetary policy within certain bandwidths.

The hub RTAs such as NAFTA and the MERCOSUR in this continent are expanding their relationships with other RTAs outside the regions. For example, they have a huge project on the Free Trade Area of the Americas (FTAA) which aims at a continent–wide FTA. The EU is also seeking to conclude a FTA with the MERCOSUR as its partner and therefore based on regional integration.

3. Opening eyes and breaking the pivots — Asian and Pacific Countries

With the third wave of RTAs, several regions where they had lagged behind became active in the RTA phenomenon. The best example is the **Asian–Pacific region**. The proliferation of RTAs in this region is challenging to the two pivots. However, the RTAs in this region are still needed to develop in systemic ways. The debate over RTAs in the Asia–Pacific region has further intensified since 2004. Notwithstanding the existence of sub–regional RTAs, most of the RTAs being created are on a bilateral basis.

Singapore is one of the hub countries for RTA phenomenon in this region. It has signed many FTAs with the countries in various regions. The pursuit of RTAs has got hold of Japan, too. Having sealed EPAs with Mexico and Chile, it has signed EPAs with ASEAN countries. Korea concluded FTAs with Chile, Singapore, the EFTA, ASEAN the United States and the EU. As for China, the Asia–Pacific Trade Agreement (APTA) and the Closer Economic Partnership Agreement (CEPA) with Hong Kong were signed. Furthermore, it recently signed FTAs with Chile and ASEAN. The three countries in **Northeast Asia** are recently pursuing RTAs as their main trade policies.

ASEAN is the main regional integration hub in Southeast Asia. It is a geo–political and economic organisation of ten countries located in this region. The aims of ASEAN include the acceleration of economic growth, social progress, cultural development among its members, and the promotion of regional peace. Although the members of ASEAN are known to be at different stages of economic development, success has been achieved in keeping members focussed on opening their economies. ASEAN has its own FTA (**AFTA**) which was signed in 1992. The AFTA is an agreement by the member nations of ASEAN concerning local manufacturing in all ASEAN countries.

At the broader regional level, ASEAN, China, Japan and Korea (**ASEAN + 3**) are discussing plans for an East Asian Community as a new framework for regional cooperation. The ASEAN + 3 process was institutionalised in 1999 at the ASEAN + 3 Summit held in Manila. This aims at strengthening and deepening East Asia cooperation and foresees the establishment of a region wide FTA. As for Australia and New Zealand, the relationship between them and ASEAN countries has been strengthened since 2005.

In South Asia, India has been the main focus of RTA activities. With its SAARC countries, India has signed the South Asian Free Trade Agreement (SAFTA), designed to revamp the South Asian Preferential Trade Agreement (SAPTA). The SAPTA made a distinction between the least developed countries (**LDC**) and other developing member countries. The agreement provided for special and differential treatment for the LDC members and also included a regional MFN provision. Thus, any preference extended within the SAPTA framework by a member that is not least developed to another that is also not least developed must be automatically extended to all SAPTA members.

The preferences granted by a non—LDC member to an LDC member must be automatically extended to all LDC members. As a part of the SAPTA special and differential treatment provisions, non—LDC members are encouraged to offer one—way trade preferences to LDCs. Though the actual exchange of preferences remained extremely limited under the SAPTA, the process of negotiation kept the dialogue among the member countries alive.

Within the region, the worldwide proliferation of RTAs led to the signing of the SAFTA with the ultimate objective of turning South Asia into a full—fledged RTA with internal liberalisation beginning in 2006. Focus of the SAFTA is primarily on tariff reduction and trade in goods. Trade in services are left untouched. Many critical items that are an important success of the SAFTA like formulation of rules of origin, preparation of the negative list, creation of a fund for compensating LDCs for loss of revenue from the elimination of customs duties, and the identification of areas for providing technical assistance to relatively weaker countries are left untouched.

India also has a series of bilateral RTAs of its own within the region. Furthermore, it is engaged in FTA negotiations with ASEAN and Thailand, having signed Framework Agreements with both. India has signed a partial scope agreement with Chile and MERCOSUR, as preliminary steps to FTAs.

4. Strengthening the relationships with the pivots or constructing own RTAs? – The other regions

RTA dynamics in the **Middle East** and the **African continent** show trends that are similar to those observed in other world regions, namely consolidation of existing agreements supplemented by a drive towards expansion, in many cases beyond neighbouring countries. However, their main RTAs seem to be more focused on the relationships with the two pivots of the RTA phenomenon based on historical, political or economical reasons.

The Middle East and North Africa (**MENA**) regions trade performance over the past two decades has been disappointing. MENA countries are liberalising their trade regime through various RTAs. Indeed, this has evolved into a complicated web of overlapping RTAs involving bilateral, plurilateral, sub–regional, and regional trading partners. At the regional level, the Greater Arab Free Trade Agreement (GAFTA) is the most comprehensive agreement, with regards country coverage, though a host of other sub–regional RTAs also exist. In spite of efforts to promote intra–regional trade among MENA countries, intra–MENA trade remains low. MENA countries are strengthening their economic and political ties with the EU through the negotiation and implementation of Euro–Mediterranean Agreements (EMAs). Trade relations between the EU and the Mediterranean countries are managed under the Euro–Mediterranean Partnership also referred to as the '**Barcelona Process**', which aims to create a common free trade area. As part of this process, Jordan, Egypt, Morocco and Tunisia recently signed the Agadir Agreement that committed them to an FTA in 2004.

As for the Gulf countries, the Gulf Cooperation Council (**GCC**) has established itself as a customs union and is engaged in several RTA negotiations both with regional and cross-regional partners. The GCC countries in addition to their FTA negotiations with the EU are also considering FTAs with India and China respectively.

There have been many ambitious RTAs in **Western, Southern and Central Africa.** However, these RTAs have not had positive impacts on their low level of intra-regional trade. Sometimes, they produced problems of poor implementation of several RTAs and overlapping membership. Regarding the extra-regional trade in this region, the basis of non-reciprocal preferences in the RTAs under schemes such as the GSP is changing. This shift to reciprocal preferences will soon extend to most countries with the RTAs replacing the long-standing unilateral preferences granted by the EU under its ACP policy.

The RTA strategies of **Central Asia or the CIS** countries seem to be far from strengthening the relationships with the pivots. In Central Asia, the regional structures pertaining to the Soviet era have been replaced by RTAs among the countries of former Soviet Union, as well as with their neighbours. The Commonwealth of Independent States (CIS) is a confederation, or alliance, consisting of 11 former Soviet Union States. The creation of the CIS signalled the dissoluoion of the Soviet Union and, according to leaders of Russia, its purpose was to 'allow a civilised divorce' between the Soviet Republics.

However, many observers have seen the CIS as a tool that would allow Russia to keep its influence over the post–Soviet states. Since its formation, the member states of the CIS have signed a large number of documents concerning integration and cooperation on matters of economics, defence and foreign policy. In addition to the CIS FTA and a customs union agreement, Armenia, Georgia and the Kyrgyz Republic as WTO members have notified a number of bilateral agreements between them and other regional partners. It would appear that most of the other regional countries have similar networks of bilateral RTAs in place that would give rise to considerable RTA overlapping. If that is the case, then we could expect some kind of consolidation in the future. Many other RTAs have been signed for the establishment of a free trade area or a single market in this region such as the EurAsian Economic Community (EEC/EAEC), the Central Asian Cooperation Organisation (CACO) and the Black Sea Economic Cooperation (BSEC).

There has been discussion about the creation of a 'common economic space' between some CIS countries. Although the agreement establishing Common Economic Space was signed, the driving motive of the Common Economic Space was not economy but politics. By the agreement, the Common Economic Space is a space uniting customs territories of the parties with mechanisms of economic regulation based on common principles promoting the free flow of goods, services, capital and labour with a common foreign trade policy. A coordinated taxation, monetary and financial policy is conducted in a way and within the scope necessary for promotion of fair competition and maintenance of macroeconomic stability. The ultimate goal would be a regional organisation that would be open for other countries to join as well, and could eventually even lead to a single currency.

LECTURE 5
WTO RULES ON RTAS

1. The Provisions of the WTO Agreement on Regional Trade Agreements

Excepting the case of RTAs to which one or more non-WTO member states are party, when a WTO member enters into an RTA through which it grants more favourable conditions to its trade with other WTO member parties to that agreement than to other WTO members' trade, it departs from the guiding principle of non-discrimination defined in Article I of GATT, Article II of GATS, and elsewhere. WTO Members are, however, permitted to enter into such RTAs under specific conditions, which are spelled out in three sets of rules:

- *Article XXIV of the GATT (as clarified in the Understanding on the Interpretation of Article XXIV of the GATT 1994) provides for the formation and operation of customs unions and FTA covering trade in goods.*

*— The so-called **Enabling Clause** (the 1979 Decision on Differential and More Favourable Treatment, Reciprocity and Fuller Participation of Developing Countries) refers to RTAs in trade in goods between developing countries.*

*— **Article V of the GATS** governs the conclusion of RTAs in the area of trade in services, for both developed and developing countries.*

The main provisions in Article XXIV of the GATT are as follows. First, the establishment of an RTA is acceptable under the GATT so long as its purpose is to facilitate trade within the region and **not to raise barriers to trade with outside economies.** Second, **duties and other restrictive regulations of commerce** shall not be on the whole higher or more restrictive than the corresponding duties and other regulations of commerce existing in the same constituent territories prior to the formation of the RTA. Third, duties and other restrictive regulations of commerce shall be **eliminated on substantially all trade** between the constituent territories in respect of products originating in such territories.

While an **Understanding on the Interpretation of Article XXIV** of the GATT 1994 was adopted as a part of the Uruguay Round Final Act, this Understanding by and large addresses technical issues that have surfaced in the application of Article XXIV and does not alter the fundamental approach of the GATT to customs unions and FTAs.

The official name of the **Enabling Clause** is 'the 1979 Decision on Differential and More Favourable

Article XXIV of the GATT

The Understanding

Enabling Clause

Treatment, Reciprocity and Fuller Participation of Developing Countries.' This decision by signatories to the GATT in 1979 allows **derogations to the MFN treatment in favour of developing countries**. In particular, its paragraph 2(c) permits RTAs among developing countries in goods trade. It has continued to apply as part of GATT 1994 under the WTO, and is therefore still in force. It allows RTAs among developing country Members in derogation from the MFN treatment obligation of Article I of the GATT. The conditions that RTAs under the Enabling Clause must meet are less demanding and less specific than those set out in Article XXIV of the GATT. The Enabling Clause does not direct any specific forms of RTAs, so arguably any form of RTA might be permitted under this clause. The RTAs under the Enabling Clause include COMESA, MERCOSUR and AFTA.

Non-reciprocal preferential agreements involving developing and developed countries require members to seek a waiver from WTO rules. Such waivers require the approval of three quarters of WTO Members. Examples of such agreements, which are currently in force, include the US-Caribbean Basin Economic Recovery Act (CBERA), the CARIBCAN agreement whereby Canada offers duty-free non-reciprocal access to most Caribbean countries, Turkey-preferential treatment for Bosnia-Herzegovina and the EC-ACP Partnership Agreement. The WTO tended to exclude these non-reciprocal agreements from the category of RTAs. For this reason, it has been noted that the granting of waivers for preferential agreements concluded between developing and developed countries has faced difficulties in recent years. It has been argued that given, the significant role played by them, and in accordance with the Doha Ministerial Declaration, negotiations should take into account the developmental aspects of RTAs so that any new rules on RTAs protect the interests of developing and least–developed countries.

The service field

The reasons today why various countries wish to enter into the economic groupings by RTAs go well beyond the rationale originally conceived in the early GATT days. During the course of the decades of the GATT's experience, statesmen and political leaders had learned that a number of problems are affecting trade relations that were either not conceived at all, or hardly conceived, in the GATT articles for trade in goods. The service field also became important in the international economy and trade as much as trade in goods. Recently, many RTAs deal with this subject.

Article V of GATS

As a result of the GATS, the multilateral trade system does now, for the first time, deal with RTAs extending beyond trade in goods and covering the supply of services (and, indirectly, foreign direct investments and movement of workers). **Article V of GATS** is the counterpart of Article XXIV of GATT for trade in services. Article V:1(b) of the GATS requires that an RTA should provide for **'the absence or elimination of substantially all discrimination.'** Furthermore, the footnote to the Article V requires that RTAs do have **'substantial coverage'** in terms of number of sectors, volume of trade affected and modes of supply.

Article V bis

Article V *bis*, entitled **'Labour Markets Integration Agreements'**, deals with a specific form of RTA which establishes full integration of labour markets between or among the parties to such an agreement. Such agreements give the nationals of the parties' free entry to each other's labour markets. Usually, these agreements also include provisions concerning conditions of pay, other conditions of employment and social benefits. Article V bis provides that the GATT shall not prevent any WTO Member from be an a party to such agreement provided that the agreement exempts citizens of parties to the agreement from requirements concerning residency and work permits and is notified to the Council for Trade in Services.

2. Article XXIV of the GATT 1947 - Before the Uruguay Round

By custom as well as explicit provision, certain RTAs had long been considered as an **exception to the MFN clause** in commercial treaties. However, RTAs had posed a difficult dilemma for commercial treaty draftsmen because of the danger of diluting the MFN clause. Therefore, the GATT 1947 was tolerant of the formation of RTAs. Many opinions trace its origins to the United States' aspirations to promote European integration and efforts to persuade developing countries to endorse the Havana Charter.

Up until 1995, RTAs had to conform to conditions set at the multilateral level only to the extent that they covered trade in goods. For various reasons, the creations of customs unions and FTAs have not been subject to a truly effective control by the GATT. Many

RTAs raised **serious questions** because either they excluded agriculture from coverage or were asymmetrical or did not provide for a definite and reasonable timetable for establishment of a full FTA and customs union.

Although both customs unions and FTAs in principle require the elimination of almost all trade barriers, in practice matters had worked out differently. Legal arguments had often been ignored or resulted in a stand–off without resolution. Generally, the compatibility of a customs union or FTA with the provisions of Article XXIV was examined by a working party, which reports its findings and discussions to the Contracting Parties. These reports discussed the issues, but typically did not reach firm conclusions. Until 1994, over 69 previous working parties on individual RTAs had been unable to reach unanimous conclusions as to the GATT's consistency in those agreements. On the other hand, no such RTAs have been explicitly disapproved. In conclusion, although many RTAs had been considered, **only a few had been approved by any formal action** by the GATT.

Furthermore, there were not many **disputes on RTAs in the GATT stage**. The panels of the GATT could also provide no decisions. The two banana cases regarding the EEC's import regimes are the best examples. Some issues regarding Article XXIV of the GATT were examined by the panels in the cases. For example, in considering whether the preferential treatment of ACP originated bananas was justified in terms of Article XXIV, the Panel focused on the fact that only the EEC undertook the obligation to eliminate trade barriers and the ACP countries came under no obligation whatsoever. The Panel found that a non-reciprocal agreement did not constitute an RTA as defined in Article XXIV. Although the Panel Report was brought to the Council in March 1994, it was not adopted. During this period, the EC and ACP countries applied for a waiver and it was granted in December 1994. Conclusively, it may be worth noting that these cases produced opportunities for the multilateral trade system to examine the RTA issues and Article XXIV of the GATT. However, there were limits for the GATT dispute settlement mechanism which came from systemic problems within it.

3. Article XXIV of the GATT 1994 - With the Understanding

In the GATT of 1994, Article XXIV remained unchanged, but, in some respects, its meaning was made more precise as a result of the Understanding concerning its interpretation. Furthermore, some cases in the WTO stage clarify several issues.

Compatibility of an RTA with Article XXIV of the GATT

(1) The compatibility assessment issue

One controversial issue in the past had been whether the **compatibility of an RTA with Article XXIV of the GATT** could be raised in dispute settlement systems, particularly in cases where the working party examination had been completed and no action had been taken by the Contracting Parties. The Understanding makes it clear that compliance with Article XXIV is an issue to which the WTO dispute settlement mechanism applies.

In the **Turkey - Restrictions on Imports of Textile and Clothing Products case,** in practice, the Panel ruled that the WTO dispute settlement system can examine the compatibility of an RTA with Article XXIV if the compatibility finding is a precondition to examining the legality of measures undertaken to form the RTA. Of course, the responsibility to make an overall compatibility assessment remains the CRTA's with its special procedures.

Whether this will lead to a much stricter control of FTAs and customs unions than under the GATT of 1947 has been debated. Some of the conditions imposed by Article XXIV continue to lend themselves to different interpretations or may seem too rigid. Several suggestions have been made to relax somewhat the substantive criteria or to interpret them in a more reasonable way than in the past and to strengthen the review procedure. Overall, it seems that WTO Members will enjoy a lesser margin of freedom than the Contracting Parties to the GATT 1947 when negotiating the establishment of FTAs or customs unions at the regional level or at the inter—regional level.

(2) 'Substantially all the trade' issue

Provided that the members of a prospective RTA notify WTO Members and agree to **eliminate tariffs and other restrictive regulations of commerce on 'substantially all the trade'** in products originating in their territories 'within a reasonable length of time,' they are permitted under Article XXIV of the GATT 1994 to ignore that agreement's MFN principle and to grant each other tariff preferences which need not be extended to non–RTA members (as well as, in the case of a 'customs union,' to form a common tariff wall).

The term 'substantially all trade' was not clarified enough, leaving open the question of whether such a determination should be based on trade coverage or tariff lines or some combination. For example, the question can be raised whether an RTA that excludes agriculture meets the **'substantially all trade'** requirement if agriculture is a small portion of trade between the RTA members. This ambiguity is likely to lead to loopholes, thereby contributing to exclusion in related RTAs of sensitive sectors such as agriculture. It is suggested that the notion be changed into the term 'all the trade' to avoid the loopholes. However, this idea is **too ambitious and idealistic**, and it is also **uncertain** whether a total elimination of trade restrictions will increase overall welfare.

Setting a certain percentage of liberalisation can also be considered as an alternative to clarify the term. The EU once urged 80% of all trade, but the matter has never been settled. As regards this issue, WTO members are in discussions as to whether to use a trade **volume–based test** or a **tariff–line based test.** The problem with a tariff–line based test is that parties to an RTA could liberalise a high percentage of tariff lines but still not liberalise a high percentage of trade if the tariff lines they refuse to liberalise currently constitute a large percentage of the trade between the countries in the RTA. The problem with a trade—based test is that trade volumes can fluctuate. It might also allow countries in an RTA to exclude many tariff lines from liberalisation that currently do not have much trade but might in the future were tariffs to be lowered. For these reasons, some countries are not satisfied with a quantitative test and want to at least supplement any quantitative test with qualitative factors. However, qualitative factors can also produce the similar ambiguity and some countries may suggest such factors to protect non—robust RTAs from being challenged.

The Understanding did not clarify whether the exceptions list to the 'substantially all' requirement is an exclusive list or not. Therefore, the question can be raised whether, internally, an RTA would be required (or at least permitted) to eliminate the application of trade remedy laws such as safeguards and antidumping among members. This is one of the bases for the long standing debate on the abolition of trade remedy measures between the parties of an RTA.

(3) 'Other regulations of commerce' issue

The term **'other regulations of commerce'** is found in Paragraph 5 and Paragraph 8(a)(ii) of Article XXIV. The similar term **'other restrictive regulations of commerce'** is employed in Paragraph 8(a)(i) and (b) of Article XXIV. These terms have been engaged in issues including whether the two terms are synonymous or not, and what types of regulations can be captured by them.

However, the terms 'other regulations of commerce' and 'other restrictive regulations of commerce' were **not clarified by the Understanding**, leaving open the question of whether RTA rules of origin are included within the meaning of these terms. For example, the question can be raised whether rules of origin should be included in an assessment of whether barriers to third country trade are higher or more restrictive than pre—RTA barriers or even taken into account when determining whether substantially all trade has been liberalised among RTA members.

The ambiguity of the term

Regarding the context of Paragraph 5, the Panel in the Turkey - Restrictions on Imports of Textile and Clothing Products case described that the meaning of the term 'other regulations of commerce' can include any regulation having an impact on trade. According to the Panel, the regulations are measures in the fields covered by WTO rules. For example, sanitary and phytosanitary measures, customs valuation, antidumping, technical barriers to trade; as well as any other trade related domestic regulation such as environmental standards and export credit schemes. Therefore, the incidence of other regulations of commerce affecting non—members of a customs union shall not **'on the whole'** be higher or more restrictive than those that were applicable to them prior to the formation of the customs union. On the other hand, other regulations of commerce affecting non—members of an FTA **'shall be no higher or more restrictive'** than those existing in the same constituent countries prior to its formation.

However, the definition by the Panel in the Turkey - Restrictions on Imports of Textile and Clothing Products case may be difficult to apply to Paragraph 8(a)(ii) in relation to a customs union formation. This is because customs union members will not normally agree to externally harmonise all of the regulatory measures that can possibly affect trade.

From a different perspective, this can be related to the issue of trade remedy measures in RTAs such as antidumping, which is provided in the Panel's definition. This question is about what types of regulations can be captured by the term. In spite of the Panel decision in the Turkey - Restrictions on Imports of Textile and Clothing Products case, the panels in other WTO RTA cases refused to rule on whether RTA members could be excluded from trade remedy measures. Although some scholars take the view that trade remedy measures must certainly be included in the term 'other regulations of commerce' or 'other restrictive regulations of commerce,' this is **still left as an unsolved question.**

(4) Other issues on Article XXIV and the Understanding

One of the principle objectives of the WTO Understanding with regard to Article XXIV is to resolve ambiguity concerning application of the requirement that a customs union's tariffs not 'on the whole' be higher than 'the general incidence of the duties and regulations of commerce' in the constituent territories prior to its formation. It was not clear from the text of Article XXIV what tariff rates would be used to calculate **the general incidence of duties** since countries bind their duties in GATT schedules but often apply duties which are lower than their bound duties. The Understanding specifies that **'applied rates of duty'** will be used in the calculation.

In addition, Article XXIV does not specify a method for determining the relative weight to be given to tariffs applicable to different products. The Understanding to Article XXIV establishes a mechanism for making such determinations. The Understanding also permits countries adversely affected by increases in tariff rates, and which have been unable to obtain adequate compensatory adjustments, to withdraw concessions in accordance with other applicable provisions of the GATT.

Measures otherwise GATT–inconsistent may be justified under Article XXIV if taken in the context of interim agreements leading to the establishment of customs unions and FTAs meeting the requirements. This is recognition of the fact that FTAs and customs unions cannot be established overnight. Although most FTAs and customs unions have been implemented by stages, only a few have expressly been notified as **'interim agreements.'** The number of interim agreements is much lower than one would expect it to be.

An interim agreement leading to the formation of an FTA or customs union must include a plan for its formation within a **'reasonable length of time.'** Since the parties forming FTAs or customs unions typically phase in their preferential tariff reductions over a transition period, typical FTA or customs union will technically be considered an 'interim agreement' during this period.

However, the notion of a 'reasonable length of time' was so vague as to defy meaningful enforcement. The WTO Understanding regarding Article XXIV provides that the aforementioned 'reasonable length of time' should 'exceed ten years only in exceptional cases'; and that 'where Members believe that ten years would be insufficient they shall provide a full explanation to the Council for Trade in Goods (CTG) of the need for a long period.' However, since Article XXIV requires only that constituent countries eliminate tariffs on 'substantially all' the trade between them, it seems reasonable to conclude that an insubstantial portion of inter—constituent tariffs could be eliminated over a longer than ten year period without the provision of a special justification.

LECTURE 6

NOTIFICATION AND REGULATION OF REGIONAL

TRADE AGREEMENTS

1. The obligation to notify

Paragraph 7(a) of Article XXIV of the GATT provides that the parties to an RTA will **notify the WTO** of the details of their RTA and that the WTO Members may make recommendations regarding it. Therefore, the paragraph requires WTO Members to notify an RTA covering trade in goods to the WTO in advance, but stops short of requiring advance approval to form or join an RTA. However, the time at which an RTA should be notified by Members is not precisely formulated nor homogeneously expressed in WTO rules.

In practice, many RTAs are notified when their texts have already been signed or even when the RTA is already in force. For example, **NAFTA** was signed on 17 December 1992 and entered into force on 1 January 1994. A working party to examine its consistency with the GATT was established on 23 March 1994. It has been argued that this restrains the effectiveness of the examination process. It has been suggested that the term 'shall promptly notify' and 'deciding to enter' in Paragraph 7(a) of Article XXIV of the GATT should be interpreted to mean that the **notification and submission of information** should take place, at least, **before the implementation of the RTA.**

Furthermore, a number of RTAs currently in force have not been notified to the WTO, in particular RTAs between developing countries. This is often cited as hindering any comprehensive and practice evaluation of the RTA phenomenon with the WTO system. The current practice of raising questions about non–notified RTAs during WTO meetings has been considered insufficient as a means of gathering adequate information. It has been suggested that **the possibility of counter–notification** of RTAs be provided for.

For these reasons, more effort should be made regarding the issues on the notification of RTAs to the WTO. The formulation of a principle is required so that examination and approval of RTAs is necessary prior to their coming into force, provided the examination occurs within a defined time frame.

2. Work of the Committee on Regional Trade Agreements (CRTA)

In February 1996, the WTO General Council established the Committee on Regional Trade Agreements (CRTA) with a mandate to verify the compliance of notified RTAs with the relevant WTO provisions and to consider the systemic implications of the agreements for the multilateral trading system and the relationship between them. **The establishment of the CRTA as the single body in the WTO** responsible for the examination of agreements helped streamline the examination process and provided a forum for the discussion of **cross-cutting systemic issues** which are common to most, if not all, agreements.

The establishment of the CRTA

RTAs under Article XXIV of the GATT are notified to the Council for Trade in Goods (**CTG**) which adopts the terms of reference and transfers the agreement to the CRTA for examination. The notification of RTAs under the Enabling Clause is made to the Committee on Trade and Development (**CTD**). The agreement is placed in the agenda of the CTD meeting where a debate is held, but, generally, no in-depth examination in the CRTA is requested by the CTD. RTAs covering trade in services, whether developed or developing, are notified to the Council for Trade in Services (**CTS**). The CTS may decide to pass the agreement to the CRTA for examination.

The procedures of the notification and examination

The CRTA decides by **consensus**. The relevant procedural rules provide that "where a decision cannot be arrived at by consensus, the matter at issue shall be referred, as appropriate, to the General Council, the CTG, the CTS or the CTD." Besides the technical and administrative difficulties of reporting and reviewing RTAs, it is the case that an absence of consensus in the CRTA regarding a number of outstanding interpretive issues continued to delay the review process.

However, the fact that the CRTA decides by consensus does not mean that the change from GATT working parties to the CRTA is without effect. The establishment of **the permanent committee** instead of working parties provides a focus and transparency that contributes to greater expertise and consistency. The members of the CRTA will be confronted with their own jurisprudence, and more likely than not, they will have before them recurring themes. They cannot easily hide behind the argument "it was someone else's working party." The passage from working parties to the CRTA can consequently contribute to a more **coherent jurisprudence in the field of RTAs.**

The examination of an RTA in the CRTA serves two purposes: it ensures **the transparency of RTAs** and allows **Members to evaluate an agreement's consistency with WTO rules.** The examination is conducted on the basis of information provided by the parties to the RTA, through written replies to written questions posed by WTO Members or through oral replies to questions posed at CRTA meetings. Once the factual examination is concluded, the Secretariat drafts the **examination report.** Thereafter, consultations are conducted and once the report is agreed by the CRTA, it is submitted to the relevant superior body for adoption.

However, no examination report on any of the RTAs notified to the WTO has been finalised by the CRTA since 1995. The cause of this failure is based on its inability to resolve the problem of reaching consensus. This is due to several political and practical difficulties. First of all, it derives from the **possible links between the CRTA-consistency judgement and the dispute settlement process.** Many WTO Members oppose any conclusive judgement on the consistency of RTAs and they believe the judgement can be closely connected with the dispute settlement process. In addition, there are **long-standing controversies about the interpretation of the WTO provisions** against which RTAs are assessed, and institutional problems arising either from the absence of WTO rules, for example, on preferential rules of origin, or from discrepancies between WTO rules and those contained in some RTAs. Other difficulties in the examination process include the diversity of RTAs; linkages drawn by the Members among the CRTA's assessments of different RTAs; and the reluctance of the parties to many RTAs to provide information on their RTAs.

The CRTA's other two functions are **to consider how the required reporting on the operation of agreements should be carried out** and **to develop procedures to facilitate and improve the examination process.** Under reporting, the CRTA has developed a regular schedule for the submission of biennial reports that applies to those RTAs where an examination report has already been adopted. Under procedures to facilitate and improve the examination process the

CRTA has developed a standard format for the submission of agreements in the area of goods and in the
area of services.

The Committee agreed to deal with **"systemic issues"**
(questions of cross–cutting concern) under a three–pro-
nged approach, encompassing legal analyses of relevant
WTO provisions; horizontal comparisons of RTAs; and
a debate on the context and economic aspects of
RTAs. The legal analysis of WTO provisions has
underlined the divergent views that exist on the interpretation of certain elements of the WTO rules governing
RTAs. In–depth discussions have taken place on many
aspects of Article XXIV of the GATT, the Enabling
Clause and Article V of the GATS based on submissions
by WTO Members and papers by the Secretariat. The
Secretariat has compiled studies on the horizontal
comparisons of RTAs.

The
systemic
issues

3. Doha Round negotiations and Transparency Mechanism

The CRTA has enjoyed **little success so far** in
assessing the consistency of the RTAs notified to the
WTO, due to various difficulties, most of which were
inherited from the GATT years. At the time of the
launch of the **Doha Round** in 2001, the CRTA had
made no further progress on its mandate of consistency
assessment due to the endemic questions of interpretation
of the provisions contained in Article XXIV of the GATT.

The Doha
Round and
the CRTA

Several WTO Members were interested in improving the discipline of the WTO on RTAs. They submitted **a number of proposals** for this purpose and these proposals addressed a number of issues. The issues are mainly related to **improving transparency and the interpretation of the concept of 'substantially all the trade.'** Against this background, WTO Members, meeting at the Fourth Ministerial Conference in Doha, agreed to launch negotiations aimed at clarifying and improving the disciplines and procedures under the existing WTO provisions applying to RTAs, while taking due account of the developmental aspects of these agreements.

A number of proposals and the negotiations

The negotiations were conducted on two tracks: **issues of a procedural nature,** and **systemic or legal issues of a more substantive nature. Negotiations on the systemic or legal issues** have made some progress, however, the scope of issues under consideration is wide and complex; the fact that clarifying or improving WTO rules on RTAs relates to several other regulatory areas under negotiation adds to the complexity. The original deadline of 1 January 2005 was missed and the current unofficial aim is to finish the talks by the end of 2006.

Two tracks of the negotiations

Negotiations on procedural issues which are by nature less contentious have instead been very fruitful with Members reaching a formal agreement on a **Decision on a Transparency Mechanism for Regional Trade Agreement** in 2006. The main features of the mechanism include the early announcement of any RTA; guidelines regarding the notification of RTAs; the preparation by the Secretariat of a factual presentation

The Decision on a Transparency Mechanism

of RTAs to assist Members in their conclusion of a notified RTA; time frames associated with the consideration of RTAs; provisions regarding subsequent notification and reporting of notified RTAs; technical support for developing countries; and the distribution of work between the CRTA and the CTD.

The Decision was applied on a provisional basis in December 2006 while awaiting the conclusion of the Doha Round. The application of the Decision provided in due time consistent, homogeneous and objective information on the RTAs notified to the WTO. However, the application showed **some problems**. Although a number of factual presentations have been prepared and used as the basis for the consideration of RTAs in the CRTA, the Committee has experienced some difficulties in adhering to the work programme established in March 2007. This was due to several factors including delays in the receipt of statistical data from parties, data discrepancies in Members' submissions, and delays in receipt of comments from parties. This has resulted in a postponement of the consideration of several RTAs. Some developing Members have faced particular technical difficulties as recognised in the Transparency Mechanism.

Nevertheless, transparency is **the first step** in unravelling the global puzzle of RTAs. It will equip Members with the necessary tools to better address **the systemic relationship between RTAs and WTO rules.**

LECTURE 7
RTA CASES IN WTO DISPUTE SETTLEMENT
SYSTEM - 1

1. Overview of the WTO cases regarding RTAs

Beside **the works of the CRTA,** one might begin to outline the features of an interpretive framework for Article XXIV of the GATT as some WTO cases have gone through **the review of the dispute settlement system.** That is to say, the considerations in both the CRTA and the dispute settlement system may give rise to certain **positive extensions of WTO case—law development** on RTA issues. Therefore, it is worth researching these WTO cases on RTAs.

Nevertheless, WTO Members have on a **small number of occasions** challenged the consistency of an RTA with multilateral rules before a panel. Most of these cases regard Article XXIV of the GATT. There are **possible reasons why WTO members refrain from challenging RTAs** before a panel. Firstly, all WTO members have now concluded RTAs and no one sees an interest in clarifying or tightening the rules under Article XXIV as this might work against one's own RTA programmes. Secondly, a WTO member may not trust panels to make binding decisions on the economically complex question of Article XXIV compliance. Thirdly, if an RTA does not liberalise 'substantially all trade' within the region and thereby violates Article XXIV, third parties may not have an incentive to challenge this inconsistency as the most logical result would be more discrimination rather than less discrimination.

Beside the attitudes of WTO members, where Article XXIV of the GATT is raised as a defence, **dispute settlement bodies** in the WTO try to avoid it in many cases. For example, the Panel and Appellate Body in Turkey–Restrictions on Imports of Textile and Clothing Products case simply presumed that the customs union between the EC and Turkey meets Article XXIV of the GATT. In many cases regarding RTAs and the Safeguards Agreement, the Appellate Body has managed to **avoid any ruling under Article XXIV on the question** of non–application to imports from within an RTA.

2. Turkey–Restrictions on Imports of Textile and Clothing Products case

The Turkey–Restrictions on Imports of Textile and Clothing Products case was **the first case** in which the WTO dispute settlement bodies affirmed the justifiability of Article XXIV of the GATT and acknowledged the competence of panels to judicially review the measures under an RTA. Although many dispute cases regarding RTAs in the WTO system are related with the trade remedy issues, this case does not deal directly with any of the three trade remedy measures. However, **the important interpretations on the formation of the customs union** in this case have often been referred to in the following cases on trade remedy measures in RTAs.

The first case on the issue of RTAs

Turkey began gradually aligning its customs duties with the EC **Common Customs Tariff with the object of achieving a customs union** as a step towards possible EC accession. As part of the final phase of the customs union, Turkey was supposed to adopt, and did apply as of 1 January 1996, relevant EC regulations regarding textiles and clothing, including certain quantitative restrictions. India argued that Turkey's quantitative restrictions on certain textile and clothing imports from India, which violated Article XI and XIII of the GATT, and Article 2.4 of the Agreement on Textile and Clothing (ATC), were not justified by Article XXIV of the GATT. The panel and the Appellate Body found that Turkey's violation of GATT and the ATC articles were not justified by Article

Turkey–EC Customs Union

XXIV of the GATT.

The Appellate Body in this case revealed that **Paragraph 5 of Article XXIV allows for violation of other GATT provisions under certain conditions**: only if the measure is introduced upon the formation of a customs union, and only to the extent that the formation of the customs union would be prevented if the introduction of the measure were not allowed. Moreover, it indicated that Article XXIV is a defence, subject to two conditions: conformity with Paragraph 8(a) and 5(a) of Article XXIV, and demonstration that the customs union would have been prevented but for the measure under discussion.

According to Paragraph 8(a) of Article XXIV, there are **two requirements to be a customs union.** First, two or more **customs territories must eliminate duties and other restrictive regulations of commerce for substantially all trade** within the customs union. The Panel and the Appellate Body commonly noted that the WTO Members have never reached an agreement on the interpretation of the term 'substantially all' but this article offers 'some flexibility' to the constituent members of a customs union when liberalising their internal trade. Second, with respect to trade barriers against third countries, the Panel and the Appellate Body also noted that **the GATT does not require that they must be the same, only that they are 'substantially the same',** affording limited flexibility to customs union members under this Article as well.

The Appellate Body noted that a customs union under Article XXIV must also meet the requirements of Paragraph 5(a) of Article XXIV. As researched above, the precise meaning of these requirements namely that the duties and 'other regulations of commerce,' applicable after the formation of the customs union, are, **on the whole, not higher or more restrictive than the general incidence of the duties and other regulations of commerce applicable prior to the formation of the customs union,** has been controversial. According to Paragraph 2 of the Understanding on the Interpretation of Article XXIV, the general incidence of duties before and after the customs union will be based upon an overall assessment of weighted average tariff rates and of customs duties collected. With respect to the term 'other regulations of commerce,' according to the Appellate Body, the Understanding indicates that "for the purpose of the overall assessment of the incidence of other regulations of commerce for which qualification and aggregation are difficult, the examination of individual measures, regulations, products covered and trade flows affected may be required."

In this case, Turkey argued that, unless it was allowed to introduce quantitative restrictions on textile and clothing from India, it would be prevented from forming a customs union with the EC. Turkey's exports of these products accounted for 40% of Turkey's total exports to the EC. Therefore, Turkey expressed strong doubts as to whether the requirement of Paragraph 8(a) of Article XXIV, namely that **duties and 'other restrictive regulations of commerce'** be eliminated with respect to **'substantially all trade'** between Turkey and the EC could be met if 40% of Turkey's total exports to the EC were excluded.

The Appellate Body rejected this argument, pointing out that alternatives to quantitative restrictions, such as rules of origin, could be used to avoid trade diversion. However, this position of the Appellate Body is questionable on two grounds. First, rules of origin can be regarded as restrictive regulations of commerce that members must eliminate under Paragraph 8(a) of Article XXIV constitute a customs union. Second, requiring customs union members to employ rules of origin keeps them from adopting one shared commercial policy and thus creates a barrier to establishing an advanced customs union.

While the status of a WTO Member remains unchanged by the mere fact that it becomes party to an FTA, the legal standing of WTO Members which become parties to a customs union seems less clear. The question is whether in the latter case WTO obligations continue to subsist and operate at the level of the original customs territories. It has been argued that a new legal entity is created when customs territories form a customs union, on the ground that a new commercial policy *vis–à–vis* third countries is then to be established. In this case, the Panel did not agree with the argument that a WTO right pertaining to a constituent member prior to the formation of a customs union could be 'passed' or 'extended' to other constituent members.

Arguably, the Appellate Body in this case established a requirement that panels must undertake a compatibility assessment of an RTA when a member is seeking to invoke the Article XXIV defence. Although this ruling may have institutional implications on the CRTA, questions can be raised regarding the functions of the institution. For example, if the CRTA does not form an affirmative recommendation regarding the compatibility of an RTA with the requirements, **the systemic problems** may emerge in the WTO stage. It means that "such a non—decision can no longer be presumed to grant a self declaratory avenue" for obtaining the benefit of the exception. However, this requirement has not been fulfilled by panels themselves in other cases. **Panels have avoided this assessment or just presumed the compatibility in many cases.**

3. Argentina—Safeguard Measures on Imports of Footwear case

This dispute concerned **the application of safeguard measures on imports of footwear by Argentina.** In 1998, the EC alleged that the safeguard measures violated the articles of the WTO Safeguards Agreement and Article XIX of the GATT. The Panel found that Argentina's measure was inconsistent with Articles 2 and 4 of the Safeguards Agreement. The Appellate Body also upheld the panel's finding, but reversed certain findings and conclusions of the Panel in respect of the relationship between the Safeguards Agreement and Article XIX of the GATT and the **justification of imposing safeguard measures only on non—MERCOSUR third country sources of supply.**

The case on the safeguard and the RTA

Regarding RTAs, non-application of safeguard measures for intra-trade of the customs union was disputed. In this case, the EC took issue with the fact that the Argentine government had concluded an analysis on the basis of figures for all imports from the MERCOSUR countries and from the non-MERCOSUR countries while applying the safeguard measure only with respect to non-MERCOSUR countries. This pattern was repeated in several other WTO cases on RTAs.

In this case, the essential question on RTAs arose **whether Paragraph 8(a) of Article XXIV prohibited Argentina, as a member of MERCOSUR, from imposing safeguard measures on other MERCOSUR countries.** It was related to **the interpretation of Article 2 and its footnote of the Safeguards Agreement.** The footnote provides:

A customs union may apply a safeguard measure as a single unit or on behalf of a member State. When a customs union applies a safeguard measure as a single unit, all the requirements for the determination of serious injury or threat thereof under this Agreement shall be based on the conditions existing in the customs union as a whole. When a safeguard measure is applied on behalf of a member State, all the requirements for the determination of serious injury or threat thereof shall be based on the conditions existing in that member State and the measure shall be limited to that member State. Nothing in this Agreement prejudges the interpretation of the relationship between Article XIX and paragraph 8 of Article XXIV of GATT 1994.

The Panel examined the meaning of the footnote and assumed that the **"footnote does not concern to whom but rather by whom a safeguard measure may be applied."** Furthermore, the Panel stated that a member–state–specific investigation cannot serve as a basis for imposing a safeguard measure on imports only from third–country sources of supply. However, the Appellate Body reversed the legal reasoning and findings of the Panel relating to the footnote, having found that the footnote is not applicable in this case.

As regards the interpretation of Article XXIV of the GATT the Panel in this case did not agree with the argument by Argentina that certain regulations prohibited Argentina from imposing safeguard measures on other MERCOSUR countries. On this issue, the Appellate Body indicated that **Article XXIV may justify a measure which is inconsistent with certain other GATT provisions** as the conclusion of the Turkey–Restrictions on Imports of Textile and Clothing Products case. Nevertheless, it noted that the analysis of Article XXIV by the Panel was not relevant in this case because Argentina did not argue Article XXIV before the Panel as a defence. For this reason, the Appellate Body also reversed the Panel's legal findings and conclusions relating to Article XXIV of the GATT. However, **Argentina took issue with Article XXIV of the GATT in the Panel stage and this point may be one of the main targets of criticisms.**

Therefore, it seems that the difficulty for the Panel was a use of Article XXIV that would allow customs union members to contribute to an injury that would then be remedied only by non–member countries.

Instead of the examination of Article XXIV, the concept of parallelism emerged in this case. The Panel firstly revealed that there had to be a parallelism between the scope of a safeguard investigation and the scope of the application of a safeguard measure. The Appellate Body also pointed out that **lacking parallelism** between them, Argentina's investigation could not serve as a basis for excluding imports from MERCOSUR member countries from application of the safeguard measure.

After all, the conclusion of **the Appellate Body relied on the concept of parallelism without the examination of Article XXIV of the GATT** in this case. It actually avoided the questions on Article XXIV. The Appellate Body also underscored that it made no ruling on whether, as a general principle, a member of a customs union can exclude other members of that customs union from the application of a safeguard measure.

LECTURE 8

RTA CASES IN WTO DISPUTE SETTLEMENT

SYSTEM - 2

4. Three Safeguards cases involving the United States
— the principle of 'Parallelism'

Although it was not one of the main issues, the WTO Panel on the US–Definitive Safeguard Measures on Imports of Wheat Gluten from the EC case considered the point of RTAs. The dispute in this case concerned the imposition by the United States of a safeguard measure on certain imports of wheat gluten. On 1 October 1997, the United States government initiated a safeguard investigation into certain imports of wheat gluten and imposed definitive safeguard measures in the form of a quantitative limitation on imports from the EC in June 1998. The EC alleged that the safeguard measures by the United States violated the articles of the Agreement on Safeguards, the Agreement on Agriculture and the GATT. Regarding RTAs, the issue in this case was focused on the imports from Canada. Although

The wheat gluten case

the imports from all sources were included in the safeguard investigation procedure, the imports from Canada (one of the United States' NAFTA partners) were excluded from the application of the measure. The EC asserted that this constituted a breach of the principle of parallelism that was recognised in the Argentina–Safeguard Measures on Imports of Footwear case. The examination of Article XXIV of the GATT could be an issue in this case. The Panel also stated that Article XXIV may provide a defence to a claim of violation of a provision of the GATT. However, the Panel did not examine whether Article XXIV might provide a defence to a violation of a provision of the Safeguards Agreement, given that such an argument had not been presented by the United States.

The Panel reached its **conclusion based on the principle of parallelism.** The Appellate Body, reaffirming the principle of parallelism, upheld the Panel's finding that the United States acted inconsistently with its obligations under articles of the Safeguards Agreement, by excluding imports from Canada from the application of the safeguard measure, after conducting an investigation embracing imports from all sources, including Canada.

The Panel and the Appellate Body in the US–Safeguard Measure on Imports of Fresh, Chilled or Frozen Lamb from New Zealand and Australia case did not deal directly with RTA issues. However, it has a similar basis to the US–Definitive Safeguard Measures on Imports of Wheat Gluten from the EC case. The United States government initiated a safeguard investigation on imports of fresh, chilled or frozen lamb

The principle of parallelism in the case

The frozen lamb case

in 1998. In 1999, this government imposed a definitive safeguard measure as a form of tariff quota. In this case, although **the scope of the safeguard investigation conducted by the United States included Canada and Mexico** (the NAFTA members) **and the Caribbean countries** under the Caribbean Basin Economic Recovery Act or the Andean Trade Preference Act, **the scope of the application of the measure did not include these countries.**

When New Zealand and Australia brought the case to the dispute settlement system in the WTO, the Panel and the Appellate Body did not examine Article XXIV of the GATT. They relied on **the principle of parallelism** and found that the United States acted inconsistently with Paragraph 1(a) of Article XIX of the GATT by failing to demonstrate as a matter of fact the existence of unforeseen developments, with Article 4.1(a) of the Safeguards Agreement by making a determination regarding the domestic industry on the basis of data that was not sufficiently representative of that industry, and with Article 4.2(b) of the Safeguards Agreement in respect to causation by not demonstrating the required causal link between increased imports and threat of serious injury.

The principle of parallelism was repeated in the US—Definitive Safeguard Measures on Imports of Certain Steel Products case. In this case, both the Panel and the Appellate Body found that the United States violated the Safeguards Agreement by excluding its NAFTA partners from the application of the safeguard on the basis that the injury determination on which the safeguard was based took account of all imports including those from Canada and Mexico.

These three cases involving the United States have several **common points in relation to the RTA issues.** Firstly, **the frames of the cases** are similar to each other. That is, whether the United States was permitted under the Safeguards Agreement to include all imports in the investigation procedure and to exclude a certain country or countries from the application of the safeguard measures. This is a similar pattern to the Argentina–Safeguard Measures on Imports of Footwear case. Secondly, the panels in these cases also reached a similar conclusion based on **the concept of parallelism.** Therefore, they seemed to rely on the panels' decisions of the Argentina–Safeguard Measures on Imports of Footwear case. Lastly, these cases are **commonly about the exclusion under an FTA** (NAFTA). One or two NAFTA members were excluded from the safeguards applications. Considering the Argentina–Safeguard Measures on Imports of Footwear case was regarding a customs union, the concept of parallelism was also applied to the FTA in exactly the same way as a customs union.

However, **the pattern in the cases and the decisions can be arguable.** Similar criticisms on the Argentina–Safeguard Measures on Imports of Footwear case are also applicable to these cases because the panels on the cases involving the United States also avoid the examination of Article XXIV. Furthermore, the concept of parallelism itself is target of criticisms.

5. US — Definitive Safeguard Measures on Imports of Circular Welded Carbon Quality Line Pipe from Korea Case

RTAs were once again one of the issues in another WTO safeguard case. The case was the US–Definitive Safeguard Measures on Imports of Circular Welded Carbon Quality Line Pipe from Korea in 2002. In this case, the safeguard measure was imposed following an investigation by the United States. In their procedures for the measure, **the imports from Canada and Mexico** (Members of NAFTA) were **included in its investigation** but they were **excluded in its application stage**. The Panel and the Appellate Body concluded that the safeguard measure of the United States was imposed inconsistently with certain provisions of the GATT and the Safeguards Agreement. Although this conclusion was not directly related with the RTAs, several arguments on RTA issues were examined in this case.

Korea asserted that the inclusion of non–NAFTA imports, but the exclusion of NAFTA imports, was **discriminatory**, and therefore **contrary to the MFN requirement** set forth in the GATT and the Safeguards Agreement. In response to this claim, the United States argued that those Articles did not prohibit a member from excluding its FTA partners from a safeguard measure because of the exception to the MFN principle set forth in Article XXIV of the GATT.

Korea argued that **Footnote 1 of the Safeguards Agreement** can be applied only to customs unions.

According to Korea, the location of the last sentence of the footnote does not make sense if it applies to FTAs. The United States disagreed with this opinion. According to the United States, the first three sentences of the footnote are about the basic question of the relationship between Article XXIV of the GATT and the Safeguards Agreement, as applied to customs unions. Furthermore, the United States asserted that any provisions of the Safeguards Agreement cannot nullify the effect of Article XXIV of the GATT, because of the last sentence of the footnote.

On this issue, the Panel agreed with the position of the United States. The Panel stated that "even though the first three sentences of Footnote 1 address the application of safeguard measures in the context of a customs union, the broader reference in the last sentence to Paragraph 8 of Article XXIV of the GATT extends the coverage of that last sentence to **include the application of safeguard measures in the context of an FTA**."

On the other hand, Korea insisted that NAFTA had not been demonstrated to be in compliance with Article XXIV of the GATT because the preliminary analysis of **the CRTA was still considering the question and a final decision on that matter had not yet been issued until that time.** The Panel rejected this Korea's claim. The Panel notes that this argument was based on the premise that an RTA is presumed inconsistent with Article XXIV until the CRTA makes a determination to the contrary. They added that there was no basis for such a premise in relevant provisions of WTO agreements. Accordingly, the Panel concluded that the

United States was permitted to rely on Article XXIV as a defence against Korea's claims.

The Panel's conclusion is challengeable in relation to the functions of the CRTA and the obligation of notification. Although NAFTA had to be notified by the WTO rule, the member countries of the FTA neglected their obligations for a long time. Accordingly, **the CRTA could not examine the compatibility of NAFTA with Article XXIV.** Therefore, the NAFTA members had to take responsibility their negligence of the obligation. However, the Panel seemed to ignore the obligation or the negligence.

Furthermore, the Panel noted that FTA members are authorised under Article XXIV, provided the relevant conditions are fulfilled, to eliminate 'duties and other regulations of commerce on substantially all the trade' between them and their FTA partners. The Panel added that those **relevant conditions were met in this case because the United States successfully demonstrated that NAFTA complied with Article XXIV and eliminated duties and other restrictive regulations of commerce on 'substantially all' trade** between NAFTA members.

It seems that the Panel's examination of the compatibility of NAFTA with Article XXIV is based on the establishment of the Appellate Body for the Turkey–Restrictions on Imports of Textile and Clothing Products case. However, the compatibility assessment is one of the main functions of the CRTA and panels must not take the role ignoring this function of the CRTA. If panels take the responsibility ignoring the work of the CRTA, many countries will not notify their RTAs to the CRTA, preferring panels. Then, the systemic relations between the CRTA and the dispute settlement system in the WTO may be in serious or complicated situations.

The Appellate Body examined the findings of the Panel on **the ground of the principle of parallelism**. The Appellate Body noted that the United States considered imports from all sources in its investigation including imports from Canada and Mexico but they were excluded from the application of the measure. The Appellate Body accepted, therefore, there was a gap between imports covered under the investigation performed by the United States and imports falling within the scope of the measure.

However, the Appellate Body reversed many findings of the Panel on RTAs and **avoided determining whether Article XXIV of the GATT** permits exemptions from safeguard measures by an FTA. According to the Appellate Body, it was not needed to address the question whether an Article XXIV defence is available to the United States. Furthermore, the Appellate Body added that it is not required to make a determination on the question of the relationship between Article XXIV and Article 2.2 of the Safeguards Agreement in this case.

The conclusion of the Appellate Body based on **the concept of parallelism can be criticised** like the conclusions of the other RTA cases based on parallelism. Conclusively, the concept of parallelism has been used by many panels on the RTA cases as the main route to avoid RTA issues.

6. Two cases on Domestic regulations under RTAs – NAFTA and MERCOSUR

Although they are not regarding trade remedy measures, there are two further cases on RTAs. The issues of the cases are certain domestic regulations under RTAs. The Canada – Certain Measures affecting the Automotive Industry case concerned itself with **the Canadian domestic acts on the automobile industry.** The Canadian measure under discussion in this case was **duty-free treatment provided to imports of motor vehicles** by certain manufacturers under the Canadian domestic orders in accordance with its obligations **under the Canada-US FTA (CUSFTA) and NAFTA** which reaffirmed the CUSFTA rule on this issue.

In 1999, the EC and Japan took this issue in the WTO dispute stage and argued that the Canada-US Auto Pact was designed to be discriminatory and was inconsistent with certain GATT articles, the Agreement on Trade-Related Investment Measures (the TRIMs Agreement), **the Agreement on Subsidies and Countervailing Measures and the GATS.**

Regarding RTAs, Canada argued that Article XXIV of the GATT grants duty-free treatment to products of NAFTA partners as an exemption from the principle of Article I of the GATT. However, the Panel stated that Article XXIV cannot justify the inconsistency with Article I of the import duty exemption made pursuant to the measure in this case. On the other hand, the United States as the third party, claimed that Article V of the

GATS can be applied to the extent of more favourable treatment to service suppliers of the United States. The Panel stated that it is not within the purpose of Article V to provide legal coverage for the extension of more favourable treatment only to a few service suppliers of NAFTA countries on a selective basis.

For these reasons, the Panel in this case found that Canada acts inconsistently with regard to some GATT articles and the inconsistency of these measures **cannot be justified by Article XXIV of GATT and Article V of GATS.** The Appellate Body also upheld the decisions of the Panel on this issue.

Most recently, the Panel and the Appellate Body in the Brazil–Measures Affecting Imports of Retreaded Tyres case avoided any examination of the MERCOSUR imports under Article XXIV of the GATT. This case was concerned with **the Brazilian domestic regulation of imports of retread tyres.** The issues in this case were the import ban and **the MERCOSUR exemption** by the regulation. The EC, the complainant, separated these two issues. Regarding RTAs, the EC claimed that the exemption from the import prohibition on retread tyres originating from MERCOSUR countries was inconsistent with articles of the GATT and could not be justified under either Article XXIV or the Enabling Clause. Brazil referred to a MERCOSUR ruling to excuse the exemption for MERCOSUR imports which the EC claimed to be inconsistent with the WTO rules.

The Panel concluded its examination on these issues in 2007. In its conclusion, the Panel found the import ban and the regulation to be **inconsistent with articles of the GATT.** On the RTA issue, the panel avoided

examining weather the MERCOSUR exemption can be issue
justified under **Article XXIV or the Enabling Clause**.
Instead of that, the Panel recognised that "the MERCO–
SUR exemption is foreseen in the very legal instrument
containing the import ban." It then included the exe–
mption issue in its analysis of Article XX regarding the
import ban issue.

The Panel exercised judicial economy in respect of
the MERCOSUR exemption issue. According to the
Panel, the exemption derived from and existed only in
relation to the import prohibition. It reasoned that the
EC's claims regarding the exemption was unnecessary
because it had already found that the import ban was
inconsistent with the articles of the GATT. The Appellate
Body also supported the Panel's view and avoided
examining separately the exemption issue. The Appellate
Body stated that it was not necessary to rule on the
MERCOSUR exemption issue upholding the Panel's
finding on this issue.

These two cases are not on trade remedy measures
and RTAs are not treated as a main issue, too. Furthe–
rmore, the panels in these cases did not provide rema–
rkable decisions on Article XXIV.

LECTURE 9

REGIONAL TRADE AGREEMENTS OF CHINA

1. RTA Policy of China

Since China implemented policies of **reform and openness** to the outside world, China has experienced **the shift of the economic system** from a planned economy into a market driven economy. Now, China is one of the major players in global trade, while already deeply integrated into the present world economy. Especially, with **the WTO accession** of China in 2000, a number of factors highlight the importance of its deep integration into the world economy. Although the main source of controversy is China's incomplete compliance with its WTO accession obligations, this situation presents both opportunities and challenges for the world economy as well as the neighbouring countries in the Northeast Asian region.

China pushed its RTA with other countries after it became a member of the WTO. The Chinese government realised that RTAs are a **useful instrument for both economic benefits and international politics**. It is

The reform and open of China

The strategic objectives of the

committed to accomplishing the following **strategic objectives** through implementing RTAs: **create stable relations with neighbouring countries; explore new markets to avoid the troubles of MTAs; provide the critical strategic resources required for economic development; push Chinese enterprises 'to go abroad' on the RTA platform; enhance the overall competitiveness of domestic industries via reasonable competition, and resolve the issues of its market economy status with RTAs.**

China has signed so far Closer Economic Partnership Agreements (CEPAs) with Hong Kong and Macao, FTAs with Chile, Pakistan, and ASEAN. The Chinese are also negotiating with Australia, New Zealand, the GCC, Iceland, and Singapore on RTAs. China is undertaking joint studies with Korea, Japan, India, South Africa and Brazil. It also agreed to pursue an RTA among the Shanghai Cooperation Organisation (SCO) members by 2020. Chinese counterpart nations include a wider range of countries around the world. This shows that China is using the RTA as a worldwide mean of international politics. It seems that one of the Chinese goals for RTAs is to build its position as a leading nation in world politics.

RTAs of China

ASEAN–China FTA	Under Implementation
Asia–Pacific Trade Agreement	Under Implementation
East Asia FTA (ASEAN+3)	Proposed / Under consultation and study
East Asia Summit FTA(ASEAN+6)	Proposed / Under consultation and study
New Zealand–China FTA	Framework Agreement signed
China–Australia FTA	Framework Agreement signed
China–Chile FTA	Under Implementation
China–Gulf Cooperation Council FTA	Under Negotiation
China–Hong Kong CEPA	Under Implementation
China–Iceland FTA	Framework Agreement signed
China–India RTA	Proposed / Under consultation and study
China–Japan–Korea (CJK) FTA	Proposed / Under consultation and study
China–Korea FTA	Proposed / Under consultation and study
China–Macao CEPA	Under Implementation
China–Norway FTA	Proposed/Under consultation and study
China–Pakistan FTA	Under Implementation
China–Peru FTA	Proposed / Under consultation and study
China–Singapore FTA	Under Negotiation
China–South AfricaFTA	Proposed / Under consultation and study
China–South African FTA	Under Negotiation
China–Thailand FTA	Under Implementation
Shanghai Cooperation Organization	Proposed / Under consultation and study

The roadmap presented by the Chinese government in 2005 indicates the major goals of China's RTA policy. First, China plans to play a **leading role in building an East Asian Economic Integration Body.** By accelerating the FTA with ASEAN and deepening CEPAs with Hong Kong and Macao, China wants to develop a China–oriented economic cooperation structure in the region. Furthermore, the economic cooperation dependent on the Chinese leadership in this region

The roadmap

could fulfil China's other objectives involving security and the resolution of disputes with its neighbours in the region. This is also important to China as it is in competition with Japan for the leadership of the region.

Second, **promotion of the Northeast Asian RTA will benefit the development of the Northeast Asian region and China.** The benefit of the CJK FTA is clear for China in this sense. Third, by promoting RTAs with Russia, Australia, the Middle East, Middle Asia, Africa, and South America, China plans to secure **a stable supply of resources and energy.** Since China is experiencing a shortage of energy due to its uncontrollable growth, energy security is one of China's major national agendas. RTAs with the GCC and Russia reflect this side of the strategy.

Fourth, China wants to **expand its market around the world** by forming RTAs. Chinese competitiveness in cheap manufacturing goods and agricultural products would allow its international market to expand as a result of the RTA. From the perspective of world politics, China seems to be planning a path to major hegemony against the United States using RTA policy. The diversity of RTA counterparts around the world indicates the importance of non—economic factors in Chinese RTA policy making.

2. Asia—Pacific Trade Agreement (Bangkok Agreement)

China, India and four other members of the **former Bangkok Agreement** renamed the group into the Asia—Pacific Trade Agreement (**APTA**) and agreed to offer up to 4000 tariff concessions among members in 2006. Korea, India, Bangladesh, Laos and Sri Lanka are the Bangkok Agreement's founding members. China acceded in 2001. Signed in 1975 as an initiative of the UNESCAP (United Nations Economic and Social Commission for Asia and the Pacific), the Bangkok Agreement is Asia's oldest RTA. The Bangkok Agreement was also hitherto called the first agreement on trade negotiations among developing member countries of the ESCAP.

The aims of the APTA are to **liberalise and expand trade; provide tariff and non—tariff concessions between member countries; give special and differential treatment to the least developed countries; and serve as a platform to link sub—regional RTAs.** Recent measures to revitalise the agreement were the amendment of the agreement; launching of several rounds of negotiations to deepen and widen the concessions available under the agreement; expansion of membership; establishment of a ministerial council; and engagement of the business sector.

Throughout its history the APTA from the Bangkok Agreement has shown a less than satisfactory trade performance. However, **China's accession** should be regarded as a major step forward for the agreement. First, China is one of the major traders in the world economy. Further, the combined populations of member countries of about 2.5 billion people make the APTA the largest RTA in the world in terms of population. With the presence of several major economies in the agreement, particularly China, India and Korea, the market potential within the agreement is huge. China's entry into the agreement has therefore brought with it several interesting possibilities and could have profound implications for trade in the region.

3. China–ASEAN FTA

In November 2001, China and the ten member country Association of South East Asia Nations (**ASEAN**) began negotiations to set up an FTA. One year later, a framework agreement laying out the FTA plan was signed. The objectives of this Framework Agreement were **to strengthen and enhance economic, trade and investment cooperation between China and ASEAN; progressively liberalise and promote trade in goods and services as well as create a transparent, liberal and facilitative investment regime; explore new areas and develop appropriate measures for closer economic cooperation between China and ASEAN; and facilitate the more effective economic integration of the newer ASEAN Member States and bridge the development gap among the parties to the Framework Agreement.**

The Agreement

The agreement was officially initiate process for the

The history

establishment of the China–ASEAN FTA (ACFTA) by prescribing guiding principles, a framework and a timetable. The FTA, a zero–tariff market of 1.7 billion people, has been targeted to come into force in 2010 for the six original ASEAN members and in 2015 for the other four. Implementation of the framework agreement would occur in stages. China and ASEAN are now the fourth biggest trading partners to each other.

The China–ASEAN dialogue relations were launched in 1991. China became ASEAN's full dialogue partner in 1996. The two sides established a strategic partnership for peace and prosperity in 2003. Recent years have witnessed the rapid and comprehensive growth in China–ASEAN relations, yielding fruitful results through extensive and in–depth exchanges and cooperation between the two sides in political, economic, trading, social, cultural and other fields.

The tariff concession structure of the FTA consists of a Normal Track and a Sensitive Track. It is similar to the AFTA. Its main difference from the AFTA is that, in addition to the two pillars, it includes an Early Harvest Programme. The Early Harvest Programme of the FTA covering trade in goods came into force in July 2005. Negotiations on a dispute settlement mechanism were finalised in 2004 for implementation in 2005. China and ASEAN also signed the agreement on trade in services of the China–ASEAN FTA in January 2007. The trade in services agreement under the framework agreement on comprehensive economic cooperation between China and ASEAN came into force in July 2007.

Although the FTA does not provide for antidumping

The provisions of the FTA

or countervailing measures, it set out the rules for safeguard measures in Article 9. Retaining their rights and obligations under the WTO rules, this article regulates the conditions and limitations for the application of the safeguard measures.

4. China–Hong Kong/Macao CEPA

The China–Hong Kong CEPA (The Mainland and Hong Kong Closer Economic Partnership Arrangement) was signed on 29 June 2003. A similar agreement, known as the China and Macao CEPA, was signed on 18 October 2003. The object of the two CEPAs is to strengthen trade and investment cooperation between China and Hong Kong/Macao and promote joint development of the two sides through the implementation of the following measures:

The CEPAs

- *progressively reduce or eliminate tariffs and non-riffs abifffers iffsubsrintially all the trade in goods between the two sides;*
- *progressively achieve liberalization of trade in services through reduction or elimination of substantially all discriminatory measures;*
- *promote trade and investment facilitation.*

With regard to the interpretation of Article XXIV of the GATT, **the legal status of the CEPAs are in nature FTAs** rather than customs unions, for they do

The legal status of the CEPAs

not mandate the parties to apply uniform duties and other restrictive regulations. The CEPAs cover three broad areas, that is to say, trade in goods, trade in services and trade and investment facilitation. All goods of Hong Kong/Macao origin imported into China enjoy tariff–free treatment when purchased by local manufacturers and upon the rules of origin of the CEPAs being agreed and met. Furthermore, Hong Kong/Macao service suppliers enjoy preferential treatment on entering into the Chinese market in various service areas. Several professional bodies of Hong Kong/Macao and the regulatory authorities in China have also signed a number of agreements or arrangements on mutual recognition of professional qualifications. Both sides agreed to enhance cooperation in various trade and investment facilitation areas to improve the overall business environment. The CEPA text was originally formed by six main chapters and six annexes.

The CEPAs adopt a building block approach, and the two sides have been continuously working closely to introduce further liberalisation measures. The agreed liberalisation measures for various phases of CEPA are stipulated in the CEPA legal text. As a result, the agreement has been added to by three supplements until 2006. The first supplement to the original CEPA text, named 'CEPA II', was signed on 27 October 2004. The CEPA II consists of the main text and three annexes. The second supplement to CEPA was signed on 18 October 2005. The name of this supplement is 'CEPA III' and consists of the main text and two annexes. The last supplement (Supplement III to CEPA) was signed on 27 June 2006. This supplement consists of the main text and an annex.

The CEPAs open up huge markets to Hong Kong/ Macao goods and services, greatly enhancing the already close economic cooperation and integration between China and Hong Kong/Macao. On the other hand, these CEPAs have controversial issues regarding their rules such as the total elimination of antidumping and countervailing measures.

5. China–Chile FTA

In June 2002, China proposed to Chile to initiate negotiations for the FTA. The formal feasibility study for negotiating the agreement was initiated in April 2004, which concluded with the approval to negotiate an FTA. On 18 November, on occasion of the bilateral activities of the APEC 2004 Summit, the Presidents of Chile and China announced the beginning of the FTA negotiations. The FTA was signed on 18 November 2005 at the 2005 APEC Summit held in Korea and came into force on 1 October 2006 after the approval of the Chilean Congress.

The main text of the FTA consists of 14 chapters and considers chapters on the following various matters: institutional and administrative proceedings, market access, trade remedies, rules of origin, sanitary and phytosanitary measures, technical barriers to trade, dispute settlement, and cooperation. A memorandum of understanding between the corresponding labour and social security authorities, and an agreement on environmental cooperation were also signed with the FTA.

With respect to tariff reductions, there is consensus for the immediate reduction of tariffs on 92% of Chilean exports to China, applicable as from the first day in which the agreement becomes effective. The agreement also considers tariff reductions after one, five, and ten years for Chilean products accessing China, and terms of one, two, five, and ten years for Chinese exports to Chile. The Chinese products that have immediate access to the Chilean market include machinery, computers, vehicles, DVDs and printers, among others.

The certificates of origin are the responsibility of government bodies of both countries. Moreover, within a period of two years, both countries will implement an electronic certification system that will improve the processes' efficiency. In the field of trade remedies, a bilateral safeguard was agreed to allow both countries to protect themselves in the event of potential increases of exports from other countries which could distort or which could have negative effects threatening the local industry. Both parties also maintain their respective rights before the WTO in terms of safeguards and antidumping.

Chapter 6 of the FTA sets out the rules for trade remedy measures. This chapter consist of two parts with nine articles. Section 1 (Article 44 to 50) provide the conditions, procedures and compensations of bilateral safeguard measures with deficedions. Section 2 (Article 51 to 52) are on the other trade remedy measures such as global safeguards, antidumping and countervailing measures.

The chapter of the agreement on sanitary and phytosanitary measures (SPS) is based on the disciplines of the SPS agreement of the WTO and is aimed at facilitating trade between China and Chile. The agreement considers the creation of a committee as the relevant forum for solving issues which may arise in relation to this topic. The agreement also ensured that technical regulations and product standards of the two nations do not create unnecessary obstacles.

It was agreed to include an expeditious mechanism on dispute settlement that allows both parties to resolve their trade quarrels within the FTA system. The agreement includes cooperation in the following areas: economic cooperation; research, science and technology; education; small and medium size enterprises; cultural cooperation; intellectual property; investment promotion; mining and industrial cooperation. It also includes an explicit reference to the agreements on labour and social security cooperation.

6. China–Pakistan FTA

The China–Pakistan FTA was signed on 24 November 2006. In April 2005, the Chinese Premier and the Pakistani Prime Minister jointly announced the launching of the negotiations on the FTA. Over the past year and a half, China and Pakistan have had six rounds of negotiations on market access for goods,

The
Agreemet

rules of origin, trade remedies, sanitary and phytosanitary measures, technical barriers to trade, investments,
dispute settlement, and consensus was reached recently. This FTA also covers the area of trade in services.

This agreement is the third FTA that has been
reached between China and foreign countries after
the China—ASEAN FTA and the China—Chile FTA. It
will further upgrade bilateral trade and economic cooperation, inject new vigour into the traditional friendly
relations between China and Pakistan, and serve as
a model for China to carry out the mutually beneficial
opening—up policy and build a harmonious world.
Like the China—Chile FTA, the agreement has a massive volume of 12 chapters as a main text.

According to the agreement, China and Pakistan
will begin to reduce/eliminate tariffs of all the products
in two phases. During Phase I, or within five years of
this agreement coming into force, both sides will reduce
/eliminate the tariffs of 85% tariff lines according to
different margins of preferences (MOP). The tariffs of
36% of tariff lines will be eliminated within three years
of this agreement coming into force. China will mainly
reduce/eliminate the tariffs of livestock, aquatic products,
vegetables, mineral products and textiles. Pakistan will
mainly reduce the tariffs of beef and mutton, chemicals
and machinery products.

Phase II starts from the sixth year of the agreement
coming into force. Both sides will further reduce tariffs
of the products des wilbasis of review of the implementation
of the agreement. The aim is to eliminate the tariffs of no
IThe than 90% of products, both in terms of tariff lines
and trade volume within a reasonable period of time

The
provisions
of the FTA

on the basis of friendly consultation and accommodation of the concerns of both parties.

Besides liberalisation of trade in goods, the agreement covers investments, including promotion and protection of investment, treatment of investment, expropriation, compensation for damages and losses and dispute settlement. The agreement also includes chapters on rules of origin, sanitary and phytosanitary measures and technical barriers to trade. The Early Harvest Programme between the two countries, which was put into operation on 1 January 2006, has been merged into this FTA.

Chapter 5 of this FTA provides for trade remedies. This chapter consist of only three articles (Article 25 to 27). The first two provisions for global safeguard measures or antidumping and countervailing measures are simple affirming the WTO rules. However, Article 27 on bilateral safeguard measures sets out the rule for conditions, limitations and investigation procedures.

LECTURE 10

REGIONAL TRADE AGREEMENTS OF KOREA

1. RTA Policy of Korea

Despite the worldwide trend of forming RTAs between countries, Korea turned its eyes to RTAs only after the Asian financial crisis in 1997. Korea's trade policy had been **focused on multilateralism rather than regionalism** before then. However, the **IMF crisis provided the momentum to promote regionalism** in Korea as one of the means to propel economic reform after the crisis. The Korean government recognised the importance of RTAs and built the plans to join the surge of Regionalism. They expected that RTAs can be **the vehicles for their recovery from the economic and financial crisis with their systemic reforms** in many areas including their national laws.

So far, Korea has signed several FTAs with Chile, Singapore, EFTA, ASEAN, the United States, India and the EU respectively, and the FTAs with the United States, India and the EU are awaiting

The RTA policy of Korea — the shift of the focus

a parliamentary ratification. Furthermore, several nego tiations are underway with Mexico, Canada, and Australia, etc. Negotiations with Japan have been suspended after disagreement over the coverage on agricultural products in November 2004.

RTAs of Korea

ASEAN–Korea FTA	Under Implementation
Asia–Pacific Trade Agreement	Under Implementation
Australia–Korea FTA	Under Negotiation
East Asia FTA (ASEAN + 3)	Proposed / Under consultation and study
East Asia Summit FTA(ASEAN + 6)	Proposed / Under consultation and study
India–Korea CEPA	Signed
Japan–Korea FTA	Under Negotiation
Korea–Canada FTA	Under Negotiation
Korea–Chile FTA	Under Implementation
Korea–EFTA FTA	Under Implementation
Korea–EU FTA	Signed
Korea–Gulf Cooperation Council FTA	Under Negotiation
Korea–MERCOSUR PTA	Proposed / Under consultation and study
Korea–Mexico FTA	Under Negotiation
Korea–Singapore FTA	Under Implementation
Korea–South Africa FTA	Proposed / Under consultation and study
Korea–United States FTA	Signed
Malaysia–Korea FTA	Proposed / Under consultation and study
Peru–Korea FTA	Under Negotiation
China–Japan–Korea (CJK) FTA	Proposed / Under consultation and study
China–Korea FTA	Proposed / Under consultation and study

In the initial stage, Korea pursued FTAs with countries of low economic significance. This was to minimise the possible negative influence on the national economy. **Two major reasons** can be suggested for the policy The reasons for the change of the change of trade policy in Korea. First, Korea started RTA negotiations to minimise damage to its trade as regionalism spread around the world after the launch of the EU in 1992 and NAFTA in 1994. Korea wanted **to avoid remaining an outsider in the worldwide trend of regionalism.** It adopted the RTA policy to maintain its market on the one hand, and move into a new market on the other. The second goal of its RTA policy was to strengthen economic competitiveness and improve its national economic system through the opening of its market and liberalisation. Korea intended **to utilise RTAs in promoting qualitative growth of the Korean economy and leaping into a more advanced economy.**

Korea has **four strategies in pursuing RTAs** with other countries. First, it pursues **simultaneous RTA negotiations** with interested counterpart countries. This is to overcome the delay in RTA competitiveness over the last 15 years and thereby to minimise the cost born by Korean companies and eventually by the Korean economy. Second, Korea seeks **a comprehensive RTA in terms of coverage and co-ntent.** Its agenda includes trade in goods, trade in services, investment, government procurement, technical barriers and intellectual property, in order to attain a higher level of RTAs which would make up for multilateral liberalisation and help domestic economic reform. Third, the Korean government takes **national consensus** building and a **transparent process** as important factors to consider as it promotes RTAs. Fourth, Korea drives **RTAs with large economies** such as the US, the EU, ASEAN and Japan. It will

Four Korean strategies in pursuing RTAs

also promote RTAs with newly rising economies such as MERCOSUR and India.

2. Korea—Chile FTA

The Korea—Chile FTA is **the first FTA** for Korea. The road toward an FTA taught Korea some hard lessons. On the one hand, the government faced **domestic opposition** and on the other, it had to resolve issues of disagreement with the counterpart country. In preparing for a future FTA, it is important to gain a thorough understanding of the Korea—Chile FTA process, and the problems it faced from inception to its conclusion. The FTA was signed in Geneva on 24 October 2002 after six negotiations for nearly three years.

The first Korean FTA

The Korea—Chile FTA is composed of 21 chapters defining a **wide range of issues: commodity trade** (market access, preferential rules of origin, customs procedures, etc.), **investment and services, trade regulations (trade remedies, competition policy, and dispute settlement), intellectual property rights, go-vernment procurement, and sanitary and phyto-sanitary measures and technical barriers,** among others. According to the concession schedule of the FTA, each party eliminates tariffs on imports from the other party, either immediately or gradually. The parties must **abolish quantitative restrictions** that are not covered by Article 11 of the GATT, as well as other

The provisions of the FTA

non—tariff barriers including import licences. As for agricultural products, the WTO Agreement on Agriculture holds sway. The parties should provide simplified procedures for issuance and confirmation of the certificate of origin.

Both parties shall provide **national and MFN treatment to the investments** from the other party and should not set the requirement of particular nationality for senior management in order to stimulate new investment and to protect the existing investment. In the field of services, an institutional system is installed to ensure national treatment for service providers, to prohibit restrictive measures and to facilitate service trade between the two parties. This is only applicable for cross—border services and not for services that are provided by carriers residing in the other country. *(Investment fields)*

Chapter 6 and Chapter 7 of the FTA state that the parties retain their rights and obligations under WTO rules. Furthermore, the parties agreed to establish **safeguard measures applied only to agricultural products.** If severe injury or market disruption occurs or is forecast due to a surge in imports of agricultural products, the parties can impose measures necessary to address the injury by stopping the FTA tariff reduction or increasing tariffs up to the MFN rate. In order to prevent anti—competitive measures from acting as trade barriers, the parties should cooperate in the area of competition rules and regulations in various ways including exchanging related information. *(Trade remedies)*

The parties liberalised the **government procurement market,** with certain limitations. Applying the principles of MFN treatment, the FTA prohibits discri- *(Government procurement market)*

minatory conditions on priority purchase of domestic goods as well as offset practices. The parties also provided adequate and effective protection and enforcement of
intellectual property rights, including well-known trademarks.

The FTA defines processing requirements which must be conducted by the exporting country in order to benefit from tariff elimination under the FTA. General regulations on the country of origin and specific rules for each item are based on those of other FTAs, such as NAFTA and the EU-Chile FTA, and adjusted in consideration of the bilateral industrial structure and trade characteristics. The scope of the country of origin was broadly defined to provide preferential tariff treatment to a wide range of exported items from each country, while strict requirements on agricultural products' country of origin were set in order to prevent imports via a third country.

3. Korea-Singapore FTA

Negotiations for the Korea-Singapore Free Trade Agreement (KSFTA) were launched in January 2004. The negotiations on key issues were concluded in November 2004 and the FTA was signed on 4 August 2005. The FTA has been under implementation since 2 March 2006.　The agreement

In the trade of goods, 59.7% (6,724 products) of the imports from Singapore enjoy **immediate tariff elimination** in Korea upon the Korea-Singapore FTA　The provisions of the FTA coming into force. In turn, Singapore eliminated tariffs on all imports from Korea. In particular, it is noted that the FTA extends tariff concessions for products manufactured in **the Kaesung Industrial Complex and other special economic zones in North Korea** that are equal to those granted to products made in Korea (South Korea). Therefore, the FTA will enable Korea to secure foreign markets for products manufactured in areas such as the Kaesung Industrial Complex and also vitalize cooperative projects between North and South Korea.

The FTA comprises many kinds of elements for liberalisation or facilitation such as national treatment and market access for **goods, rules of origin, trade remedies, customs procedures, sanitary and phyto sanitary measures, technical barriers to trade and mutual recognition agreement, cross–border trade in services, telecommunications, financial services, electronic commerce, temporary entry of business persons, investment, intellectual property rights, competition and government procurement** with 22 chapters.

Chapter 3 sets out the rules governing **trade in goods** between Korea and Singapore. These rules are based on WTO disciplines and contain WTO–plus provisions. Both countries will grant preferential tariff–free market access for an extensive range of products. The chapter also provides for possible acceleration of tariff elimination or inclusion of additional products for tariff elimination in the future. In addition, each country must ensure that its excise taxes and other charges are not levied in an unjust manner that will result in discrimination against imported products.

The chapter for **rules of origin** was negotiated on a product–specific approach. This means that each product has a corresponding specific rule of origin, to cater to the specific needs of every industry. The rules of origin of the FTA ensure that only goods manufactured in Korea or Singapore will benefit from the FTA. Goods from third countries will not be able to pass off as Korea or Singapore originating goods.

Chapter 6 sets out five articles regarding **trade remedies**. Although the FTA allows for the continued use of antidumping measures under this chapter, the provisions have been tightened to limit the amount of antidumping duties that may be imposed. Both countries are also allowed to take bilateral safeguard action of durations of not more than two years. The countries have also reaffirmed their commitments under WTO safeguards and countervailing and subsidies agreements.

Chapter 9 governs cross–border **trade in services** between Korea and Singapore. Both countries agreed to grant services and service suppliers of the other country the same treatment given to their domestic services and service suppliers. Furthermore, both countries cannot impose quantitative restrictions like limitations on the number of service suppliers or the number of service operations. There are also disciplines on domestic regulation to ensure that measures affecting trade in services are imposed in a reasonable, objective and impartial manner, as well as provisions that prevent monopolies from abusing their position.

The Korean government expects that the Korea–Singapore FTA will not only expand the trade volume between Korea and Singapore, but also strengthen the foundation for Korean industries to make **inroads into the East Asians markets**. This is an important point considering the China–ASEAN FTA, APTA and even the possibility of a China–Korea FTA. Moreover, Singapore is an international hub for business, finance and distribution and is increasingly becoming a target investment country for multinational companies. Korea hopes to advance their economic system by strengthening ties with Singapore through the FTA.

4. Korea–EFTA FTA

The FTA between Korea and the EFTA States was signed in Hong Kong on 15 December 2005. The agreement came into force on 1 September 2006. The agreement covers all major areas of trade relations including **trade in goods, trade in services, government procurement, competition and intellectual property**. A joint committee is established for the supervision of the agreement, and a chapter provides for dispute settlement procedures. Moreover, Korea and the EFTA States concluded bilateral agreements on basic agricultural products. An agreement on investment has been concluded between Korea, on the one hand, and Iceland, Liechtenstein and Switzerland, on the other, as well. The agreement consists of 10 chapters with a total of 88 articles and 13 annexes and is completed by a record of understanding.

Korea is an important trading partner of the EFTA States. Most industrial goods, including fish and other marine products, have benefited from duty–free access to the respective markets as of the agreement coming into force. For some products imported into Korea, customs duties are to be **eliminated after a transitional period** or **after a joint review** by the parties. The agreement provides for liberal rules of origin and allows for the use of up to 60% of non–originating input in the production of certain products. Similar to the Korea–Singapore FTA, the Korea–EFTA FTA extends **tariff concessions for products manufactured in the special economic zones in North Korea such as the Kaesung Industrial Complex.** Furthermore, the FTA includes three articles (Article 2.9 to 2.11) for trade remedies in Chapter 2.

The provisions of the FTA

Trade in processed agricultural products is co–vered in an annex to the main agreement. In addition, trade in basic agricultural products is covered in three bilateral agreements on basic agricultural products negotiated between the respective EFTA states, Iceland (Agricultural Agreement between Iceland and Korea), Norway (Agricultural Agreement between Norway and Korea) and Switzerland/Liechtenstein (Agricultural Agre–ement between Switzerland and Korea) and Korea. These agreements form part of the FTA.

Trade in processed agricultural products

Trade in services is covered in Chapter 3 and in annexes on specific commitments (Annex VII), MFN exemptions (Annex VIII), mutual recognition (Annex IX), telecommunication services (Annex X), and co–production of broadcasting programmes (Annex XI). The agreement covers all four modes of delivery (supply) of a service,

Trade in services

as defined under GATS, and addresses all services sectors. As in the GATS, the positive lists of specific commitments of each party are an integral part of the agreement. These lists will be reviewed every two years (the first revision will take place three years after the agreement coming into force), with a view to providing for a reduction or elimination of substantially all the remaining discrimination between the parties for trade in services covered by the present section on services. Trade in financial services is dealt with in chapter 4, which also establishes a sub-committee on financial services. Commitments have been improved to reflect recent legislative changes by the parties.

The chapter on **competition** deals mainly with the co-operation, notification, consultation and exchange of non-confidential information between the parties. In particular, consultations are provided for when important interests of Korea or an EFTA member state may be adversely affected. In the chapter on government procurement and Annex XII, the parties recognise that the WTO Agreement on Government Procurement (WTO GPA) governs the rights and obligations of the parties in this field.

The agreement sets a **high standard for the protection of intellectual property rights** in Chapter 7 and Annex XIII, covering areas such as patents, trademarks and copyright, and goes, in certain areas, beyond what is provided for under the WTO Agreement on Trade-Related Aspects of Intellectual Property Rights (TRIPS) and other international conventions and treaties.

The agreement establishes a **joint committee**, which supervises and administers the agreement and oversees the further elaboration of the agreement. Information exchanges and consultations can take place in the joint committee. The joint committee also takes dec can s in cases provided for by the agreement or makes recommendations. Secretariats are also established under Article 8.2 of the agreement, consisting of the EFTA secretariat for the EFTA states and the Ministry of Foreign Affairs and Trade for Korea.

A chapter on **dispute settlement** contains rules and procedures for the avoidance or settlement of disputes arising from the agreement between one or several EFTA states and Korea.

An agreement on **investment** was separately co-ncluded between Korea, on the one hand, and Iceland, Liechtenstein and Switzerland, on the other. This agreement covers both access to markets and the protection of investments. The three EFTA states and Korea grant each other national treatment for the establishment of investors, except for a few cases where the parties have lodged reservations based on restrictions in their national legislation. The agreement also foresees the possibility of direct dispute settlement between an investor and the party of investment.

5. Korea–ASEAN FTA

In October 2003, at the ASEAN–Korea Summit held in Bali, Indonesia, Korea proposed that Korea and ASE-AN should deepen relations by developing a establishing an FTA. As a commitment to the realisation of this FTA, at the November 2004 Summit, the respective leaders agreed that ASEAN 6 and Korea shall eliminate tariffs for 80% of all products by 2010.

Negotiations for the Korea–ASEAN FTA commenced in 2005. The whole FTA consists of four parts as **Framework Agreement, Agreement on Dispute Settlement Mechanism, Agreement on Trade in Goods and Agreement on Trade in Services**. The FTA on the trade in goods area entered into force in June 2007, while the FTA on the trade in services area was signed in November 2007.

Four parts of the FTA

The Framework Agreement consists of 21 articles and three annexes. The part of Agreement on the trade in goods is ruled by the three annexes. Annex 1 is 'Modalities for Tariff Reduction and Elimination for Tariff Lines Placed in the Normal Track' and Annex 2 is 'Modalities for Tariff Reduction and Elimination for Tariff Lines Placed in the Sensitive Track.' Annex 3 of the FTA is about the rules of origin.

The Framework Agreement

The tariff reduction or elimination between the two Parties is categorised under four different lists by the FTA. The first list is the 'Normal Track 1.' The tariffs on the goods in this list should be eliminated by 1 January 2010 for Korea and ASEAN 6. The second list is the 'Normal Track 2.' The tariffs on the goods in this list should be eliminated by 1 January 2012 for ASEAN 6 only. The third list is the 'Sensitive List.' The tariffs on the products categorised in this list should be reduced to not more than 20% by 1 January 2012 for Korea and ASEAN 6. The last list is the 'Highly Sensitive List.' The products in this list

The tariff reduction or elimination

split into five groups with different commitments as
below:

- *Group A: Tariff rate to be not more than 50% by
  1 January 2016*
- *Group B: Tariff rate to be reduced by not less
  than 20% by 1 January 2016*
- *Group C: Tariff rate to be reduced by not less
  than 50% by 1 January 2016*
- *Group D: Application of tariff–rate quotas*
- *Group E: Products excluded from granting any
  concessions (capped at 40 tariff lines at HS 6–
  digit level)*

The Korea–ASEAN FTA will enable both economies to **reform their agricultural and industrial sectors**, and it will **create a strategic coalition** that can mitigate any adverse effects arising from the acute China–Japan rivalry in the Southeast Asian region. Despite these benefits, there are **three major challenges** facing the integration of Korea and ASEAN's economies.

First, Korea is trying to retain **trade barriers for its major agricultural products**, and ASEAN wants to retain trade barriers against some Korean exports. This mutual retainment of trade barriers might be inconsistent with WTO rules, and it would reduce the benefits of trade liberalisation, which is the purpose of the FTA. Second, not all ASEAN countries are WTO Members, and Korea may find it **difficult to obtain WTO approval for the FTA**. As a result, Korea needs to ensure that its agreements with non–WTO countries comply with WTO rules. Third, this FTA is expected to

The
opportunities
and
challenges

include **special rules of origin for a South and North Korean economic cooperation project**. In order to be compatible with WTO regulations, the FTA must ensure that the rules are used only for preferential tariff purposes.

6. Korea-US FTA

Korea concluded an historic FTA with the United States on 1 April 2007 after 10 months of tough negotiations. This Korea-US FTA was officially signed in Washington D.C. on 30 June 2007. Although the FTA has been completed and enjoys strong support from business in both countries, the ratification debate in the two countries is still contentious.

Many specialists in business area and the two governments expect that the **comprehensive trade agreement** will eliminate tariffs and other barriers to trade in goods and services, promote economic growth, and strengthen economic ties between the two countries. However, there are also many different opinions in the governments. It is controversial because the reforms required by the FTA will increase competition for the firms, workers and farmers of Korea and the United States and thus will require adjustment.

The Korea-US FTA drew **mixed reactions from the big competitors in the international economic stage**. For example, the FTA led to some arguments for the prospect of an RTA between Japan and the United States. Considering the economic effect of the

FTA, the regional rivals China and Japan may regard the Korea–US FTA as a pivot for the Korean RTA policy which makes Korea a trade hub for the two countries in Northeast Asia. Furthermore, the FTA may give a boost to Korea's credit rating and a competitive advantage over China and Japan. The FTA also accelerated the preparations and launch in May 2007 of new FTA negotiations between the EU and Korea.

The Korea–US FTA **covers all areas of trade relations including trade in goods, trade in services, investment, government procurement, competition and intellectual property** with massive text. More than 90% of all tariffs on bilateral trade will be removed within three years, which is significant even though average tariffs are relatively low, because bilateral trade is so large. Even in agriculture, where Korean trade barriers are much higher, many tariffs will be phased out over time and many quotas will be expanded; only rice will be exempted from some degree of liberalisation. Besides the tariffs cuts, the Korea–US FTA substantially reduces the burdens related to tax and regulatory policies. The FTA provisions provide greater transparency and access to the regulatory process and a dispute resolution procedure to encourage compliance. It also provides special rules for the Kaesung Industrial Complex in North Korea, like many Korean FTAs with other countries.

LECTURE 11
REGIONAL TRADE AGREEMENTS OF JAPAN

1. RTA Policy of Japan

Japan did not pay much attention to the worldwide trend of RTAs before the Asian crisis in the 1990s. Japanese government officials took the multilateral liberalisation process more seriously and disregarded the **shifting trend to regionalism**. However, the difficulties of WTO negotiations and the rising number of RTAs around the world led Japan to rethink its trade policy in favour of RTAs. Japan concluded an EPA with Singapore in November 2002 for the first time, and subsequently signed EPAs with Malaysia, Mexico, Philippines, Chile, Thailand and Indonesia, Brunei. RTA negotiations with Australia, ASEAN, Switzerland, Vietnam, India and the GCC are under progress. Joint study with Canada is still progressing.

The Japanese Regionalism and RTAs

ASEAN–Japan CEPA	Framework Agreement signed
East Asia FTA (ASEAN + 3)	Proposed / Under consultation and study
East Asia SummitFTA(ASEAN + 6)	Proposed / Under consultation and study
Japan–Australia EPA	Under Negotiation
Japan–Brunei EPA	Signed
Japan–Canada FTA	Proposed / Under consultation and study
Japan–Chile EPA	Under Implementation
Japan–Gulf Cooperation Council FTA	Under Negotiation
Japan–India EPA	Under Negotiation
Japan–Indonesia EPA	Signed
Japan–Korea FTA	Under Negotiation
Japan–Malaysia EPA	Under Implementation
Japan–Mexico EPA	Under Implementation
Japan–Philippines EPA	Signed
Japan–Singapore EPA	Under Implementation
Japan–Switzerland EPA	Under Negotiation
Japan–Thailand EPA	Under Implementation
Japan–Vietnam EPA	Under Negotiation
China–Japan–Korea (CJK) FTA	Proposed / Under consultation and study

The characteristics of Japanese RTAs are threefold. Firstly, Japan chose **ASEAN nations as a priority in picking RTA counterparts** at the early stage of RTA negotiations. Japan signed EPAs with three ASEAN member countries individually, and is and will be negotiating with four ASEAN countries. Japan has continuously expanded its investment to Southeast Asia since the 1980s and has a mutually complementary production structure with ASEAN countries. EPAs with ASEAN countries will maximise the economic benefit to Japan based on this economic relationship. On the other hand, this policy also intends to restrain rising

The characteristics of Japanese RTAs

Chinese influence in this region. This policy of Japan stimulated China to join the RTA competition in the Southeast Asian region.

Secondly, **the level of market entry in the manufacturing sector is high, while that in agriculture and fishery is relatively low.** Japan has sensitive agricultural and fishery sectors. Therefore, Japan required effective exclusion or, at least, some form of special treatment regarding these sectors in many RTA negotiations. As the results of the negotiations, Japan allows a high level of market entry in the manufacturing sector and a medium level in agriculture and fishery in its RTAs. The political influence of the agricultural sector is still high in Japan and farmers have been a major obstacle in the Japanese trade liberalisation drive.

Thirdly, Japan utilises **RTA policy as a means of not only trade policy but also regional diplomatic policy.** Japan seeks to make a favourable international political environment in pursuing its goals in the international community. In particular, Japan intends to take a leading position in the economic community in the region of East Asia, competing with China. Japanese RTA policy shows non—economic factors are more important in their policy decision—making. Maximisation of economic benefits from the formation of RTAs is not the priority of Japan. Rather, minimisation of domestic conflict and adjustment costs seem to be more important in Japan's RTA policy decision—making. Curbing China's rise in Southeast Asia seems to be another important policy goal for Japan as is shown by RTAs with major ASEAN countries. Japan's choice

for an RTA counterpart shows its interest is overwhe—
lmingly in developing countries, rather than developed
countries.

2. Japan—Singapore EPA

Negotiations for the agreement between Japan and The
Singapore for an EPA were launched on 22 October Agreement
2000. This followed the positive recommendation by
the Japan—Singapore Joint Study Group, which had
been tasked to study the proposed FTA. The agreement
was signed on 13 January 2002 in Singapore and
came into force on 30 November 2002 after legislative
processes with the respective parties.

The agreement comprises liberalisation and facilitation The
in several fields such as **trade in goods, rules of origin,** provisions
customs procedures, mutual recognition agreement, of the EPA
trade in services (including financial, courier and
telecomunication services), investment, movement
of natural persons and government procurement. It
also contains provisions for cooperation of each party,
dispute settlement and the review of the agreement.
The main text of the agreement consists of 22 chapters
with a total of 153 articles.

There are ten articles in Chapter 2 which essentially Trade in
set out the rules governing **trade in goods** between goods
Japan and Singapore. These rules are based on WTO
disciplines and serve to eradicate barriers to trade in
goods. Specifically, the chapter commits both countries

to grant preferential tariff free market access to an extensive range of products. It also provides for possible acceleration of tariff elimination or inclusion of additional products for tariff elimination in the future.

The services chapter builds on what has been accomplished at the multilateral level. The chapter consists of 14 articles that prescribe the general disciplines governing trade in services between Japan and Singapore. The sectoral commitments forming the core of the obligations are undertaken by each country. These commitments identify the services sectors for which it agrees to offer market access and national treatment. In addition, additional disciplines for financial services and telecommunications services are imposed through two separate annexes.

Japan is a key investor in Singapore. Chapter 8 consists of 19 articles that prescribe the general disciplines governing the **investment regimes** in Japan and Singapore for investors from both countries. As the aim of the investment chapter is to create favourable conditions for bilateral economic activities and to stimulate bilateral investment flows between Japan and Singapore, the chapter focuses on two key elements, comprising provisions on investment promotion and investment protection.

The cross-border **movement of business persons** plays a central role in initiating trade and investments. Chapter 9 is divided into two parts. The framework of five articles lays out the terms and extent to which the natural persons of one party, which include her citizens/nationals and permanent residents, can enter into the other party's territory for the purpose of doing business.

Article 18 of the EPA relates to the imposition, during
the transition period to the bilateral duty-free trade, of
safeguard actions by one party to the products of the
other in the event of serious injury of a domestic industry
of the first party. This emergency measure in this EPA
has several points that are different from the threshold
and methods used for safeguard actions under the WTO.

Trade remedies

3. Japan-Mexico EPA

Japan and Mexico agreed to start negotiations on
an economic partnership agreement (EPA) at the
Summit Meeting held in October 2002. In March 2004,
they confirmed that both sides reached agreements in
substance on major elements of the agreement. The
agreement was signed on 17 September 2004 in
Mexico City and came into effect on 1 April 2005.

The Agreement

Through the conclusion of the agreement, Japan
took the opportunity to gain expanded access to the
Mexican market. The main target of the agreement for
the Japanese position was the United States market
because the Japanese government thought that the
agreement may allow Japanese companies to enjoy
equal treatment with companies in the United States,
Canada and Mexico by NAFTA, in areas such as
customs duties, services, investment and government
procurement. The agreement also enables Japan to
enter the North and South American markets via

The effects and provisions of the EPA

Mexico. The agreement consists of 18 chapters with a total of 177 articles and 18 annexes.

As for trade between the two countries, **customs duties** are comprehensively eliminated or reduced. The agreement provides for the elimination of tariffs on over 90% of goods. In particular, both countries agreed to eliminate or reduce customs duties of products in the area of agriculture, forestry and fisheries, which cover almost all imports from Mexico in such areas. These agricultural products are classified according to the treatment of customs duties in such groups as; immediate elimination, gradual elimination from three to ten years, establishment of a non—taxable quota, reduction of customs duties, consultation, or exclusion form the regulation of the agreement.

With some exceptions, both countries committed to provide national treatment and MFN treatment in the fields of **investment and cross—border trade in servi— ces.** A performance requirement such as requirement for local content as a condition for investment was prohibited. Japan and Mexico also agreed to cooperate in nine areas: trade and investment promotion, suppo— rting industries, small and medium enter asses, science and technology, technical and vocational education and training, intellectual property, agriculture, tourism, and the environment.

Especially, this EPA has specific regulations on bilateral **safeguard measures** in Chapter 6. This chapter consist of six articles (Article 51 to 56) which set out the rules for conditions, proceedings and definitions. They also provide for provisional safeguard measures.

4. Japan–Malaysia EPA

The Japan–Malaysia EPA was signed on 13 December 2005 in Kuala Lumpur following nearly two years of negotiations. Malaysia is the third RTA partner for Japan following Singapore and Mexico. This agreement came into force on 14 July 2006.

It covers not only **trade in goods,** but also **services trade, intellectual property right protection, investment rules, competition policies, business facilitation and cooperation projects for personnel training in Malaysia.** Cooperation areas included are agriculture, forestry and commodities, education, human resource development, information and communication technology, small and medium enterprises, science and technology, tourism and environment. The agreement consists of 14 main chapters with a total of 159 articles and 9 annexes.

In the field of industrial products, both sides will eliminate tariffs on essentially all goods within ten years from the date of the entry into force of the agreement. The tariff concession structure of the EPA is quite complex. It consists of 15 different categories. Furthermore, the agreement also has articles regarding trade remedies including bilateral safeguard measures. Article 23 of this EPA sets out the rules for bilateral safeguard measures like many other Japanese EPAs.

The two countries recognise the growing importance of **intellectual property** protection in pursuing further promotion of trade and investment. Both sides ensure adequate and effective protection of intellectual property

The fields and the provisons of the Agreement

and provide for measures for enforcement of intellectual property rights. The agreement also provides a frame-work for further expansion and facilitation of freer cross-border investment between the two countries through commitments on national treatment, MFN trea-tment and enhanced protection of investors and inve-stment.

Japanese manufacturers will benefit from the agree-ment as it will boost their competitiveness by lowering parts procurement costs in Malaysia, while Malaysian local industries would also gain from Japan's coopera-tion programs stipulated in the accord, according to Japanese officials.

5. Japan-Chile EPA

Japan and Chile announced their intention to eval- **The** uate the possibility of negotiations towards an RTA on **Agreement** 22 November at the 2004 APEC Summit, held in Santiago, Chile. Following the evaluation of the results of the Japan-Chile Joint Study Group, the two countries announced their intent to launch FTA negotiations on 18 November 2005, in Seoul, Korea at the APEC heads of state meeting. The Agreement between Chile and Japan for a Strategic Economic Partnership was signed on 27 March 2007 in Tokyo. This Japan-Chile EPA is the first of Japan's EPAs with a South American nation and came into force on 3 September 2007.

The EPA covers a **comprehensive range of eco-**

nomic issues, including trade and investment libera—
lisation and facilitation. These are improvements of the
business environment, entry and temporary stay of
nationals for business purposes, intellectual property,
competition, government procurement, technical barriers
to trade and sanitary and phytosanitary measures.
The main text of the EPA consists of 19 chapters
with a total of 199 articles.

Section 2 of Chapter 3 in this EPA has several regu—
lations on bilateral **safeguard measures**. This section
consists of seven articles (Article 20 to 26) which sets
out rules for conditions, investigations and limitations,
consultations and compensations with provisional mea—
sures. They are similar to the articles of the Japan—
Mexico EPA.

The provisions of the EPA

LECTURE 12

VISION FOR THE CJK FTA IN NORTHEAST ASIA

The Northeast Asian Countries have lagged behind in the worldwide boom of regionalism. However, such a criticism is not at all relevant now. Despite WTO systems, trade liberalisation and economic reforms have often been undertaken by the RTAs in China, Korea and Japan. The three countries in **Northeast Asia reveal different characteristics in their RTAs.** In selecting counterparts for their RTAs, China and Japan tend to pick developing countries while Korea tends to choose advanced countries such as EFTA and the United States. These kinds of country choice patterns reflect the different goals of the three countries. Korea as a middle—ranking power in the world tends to emphasise economic benefit while China and Japan as major powers in the world tend to focus relatively more on non—economic values.

Different characteristics in The Northeast Asian RTAs

This relates to the next characteristic of RTA policies of the three countries. China and Japan seem to pursue regional hegemony in East Asia through RTA policies. Both countries took ASEAN member countries as important RTA counterparts and put higher priority

The relationship with ASEAN

on ASEAN in their RTA negotiations. ASEAN was the first FTA counterpart to China and the China–ASEAN FTA was signed in November 2004. Japan, on the other hand, put emphasis on individual FTAs with ASEAN member countries and signed FTAs with major ASEAN members. In the case of China, building a base for a world hegemonic nation competing with the United States seems to be a hidden goal of its RTA policies. On the other hand, Korea's interest as an FTA partner of ASEAN is more focused on economic benefit. Korea took its FTA initiative as a way to advance its economic system and revive from economic crisis.

In terms of fields of interest, China considers energy and resource security as one of the prime goals of RTAs around the world. Japan prefers a lower level of market entry in agriculture and fishery, while allowing high market entry in the manufacturing sector. Korea, meanwhile, pursues a comprehensive FTA including services, investment, government procu– rement, intelle– ctual property rights, and so on.

The fields of interest in the Northeast Asian RTAs

The share of intra–regional trade between China, Japan and Korea has risen substantially from 12.7% in 1990 to 23.9% in 2005. In 2006, Japan and Korea were the second and fourth largest trading partners, respectively, for China. For Japan, the second and third most important trading partners were China and Korea, respectively, after the United States. China and Japan were the first and second largest trading partne– rs, respectively, for Korea. In this situation, before and after the Asian financial crisis in 1997, there have been some attempts at economic cooperation in the region.

Intra–regional cooperation in the region

Even though China, Korea and Japan are not ready to consider formal regional economic integration, they have become interested in **the idea of forming a Northeast Asian FTA (CJK FTA).** From a long term view, the CJK FTA can be regarded as the first step for the 'Northeast Asian Community' as the ultimate vision for Northeast Asian economic integration. The scholars and governments of the countries have discussed the subject and they have proposed several ways to achieve this goal as given below:

- *Direct trilateral negotiation for the CJK FTA*
- *Bilateral RTAs and integration of the RTAs into the CJK FTA*
- *The East Asian RTA negotiation including the CJK FTA*

First of all, the three countries can consider the trilateral negotiations for the CJK FTA. Although this will be the most direct way to the goal, it has many political or other obstacles for the countries to overcome at the same time.

Instead of that, they can take two steps for the goal as a second option. In other words, they can have bilateral FTAs between two countries of the region such as the China–Korea FTA and the Korea–Japan FTA as the first step, then, integrate their FTAs to the CJK FTA as the second step. In this method, three countries can also consider one bilateral FTA of two countries and the participation of the other country in the FTA. This is similar to the NAFTA method. The CUSFTA between Canada and the United

States was developed to the NAFTA with the participation of Mexico.

Lastly, the idea of the East Asian FTA (EAFTA) or
the ASEAN+3 (China, Korea and Japan) is proposed
as the economic integration of the East Asian region.
This must be taken into account when thinking about
the CJK FTA. As researched above, the three countries
already have developed their FTA relations with ASEAN
countries in different ways. Therefore, if they harmonise
the relations by negotiations, the ASEAN+3 FTA will
be realised by the AFTA plus the CJK FTA. For
example, the tariff concession structures of the AFTA,
the ACFTA and the Korea–ASEAN FTA are basically
similar to each other as researched above. It seems
that Japan will also take this basic structure in the
Japan–ASEAN RTA (FTA or EPA) if they reach the
RTA.

Although there may be controversy on the methods
to achieve the goal, the three countries need to have
the CJK FTA now. They have agreed that the **CJK
FTA will be a win–win–win strategy** for the three
countries, bringing benefits to them all. However, they
still have many issues to discuss about the CJK FTA
in addition to **political and emotional obstacles.**
There have been several joint studies of the three
countries for these matters since 2003. The three
countries should **harmonise and overcome the
differences** for building the CJK FTA. The Northeast
Asia of the CJK FTA is possible and should be realised in the near future.

The possibility and the prospectus

INDEX

Bong—Chul Kim

▌약 력

The Author is a Lecturer at Hankuk University of Foreign Studies (HUFS) in Seoul. He completed his undergraduate degree in law at HUFS, graduating with the highest distinction. After national service as an officer in the Korean Army, he studied for his master degree on the topic of FTAs at HUFS. His research topic for the Ph.D was also RTAs at King's College London (University of London). His research was funded by an Overseas Research Students (ORS) Award of the UK government. He has worked on several FTAs research projects with the Korean Government and the Korean Legislation Research Institute (KLRI).

Lectures on FTAs and RTAs

초판인쇄 | 2009년 12월 9일
초판발행 | 2009년 12월 9일

지은이 | 김봉철
펴낸이 | 채종준
펴낸곳 | 한국학술정보㈜
주　　소 | 경기도 파주시 교하읍 문발리 파주출판문화정보산업단지 513-5
전　　화 | 031) 908-3181(대표)
팩　　스 | 031) 908-3189
홈페이지 | http://www.kstudy.com
E-mail | 출판사업부　publish@kstudy.com
등　　록 | 제일산-115호(2000. 6. 19)

ISBN　978-89-268-0674-6 93360 (Paper Book)
　　　　978-89-268-0675-3 98360 (e-Book)

내일을여는지식 █ 은 시대와 시대의 지식을 이어 갑니다.